EFFECTIVE ENGLISH

E. Suresh Kumar
P. Sreehari
J. Savithri

Longman
is an imprint of

Delhi • Chandigarh • Chennai

Credits

Unit 1: pp. 3–5: R. K. Narayan's "A Hero", from *Malgudi Schooldays: The Adventures of Swami and His Friends*, New Delhi: Penguin/Puffin, 2002; © India Thought Publications. Reproduced with permission.

Unit 2: pp. 29–31: "Marine Ecosystems", accessed from the Web site of the United States Environmental Protection Agency, www.epa.gov/bioindicators/aquatic/marine.html. Reproduced and modified with permission; pp. 36–37: Critical essay, taken from Saradindu Bhattacharya's "Harry Potter as Detective". Reproduced with the author's permission.

Unit 3: pp. 45–50: W. Somerset Maugham's "The Verger", © The Royal Literary Fund. Reproduced with permission; p. 53: Cricket drawing courtesy of Kapil Pandey.

Unit 4: p. 64: Photo of dabbawallahs © Steve Evans. Used with permission; p. 68: Photos courtesy of Kapil Pandey.

Unit 7: p. 126: Plastic bags photo © www.rentagreenbox.com. Used with permission; p. 127–29: "Perilous Plastic Bags", accessed from the Web site of the Civil Service of Pakistan, www.cssforum.com.pk/css-compulsory-subjects/everyday-science/8582-hazards-plastic-bags.html. Used with permission.

Cartoons on pages 5, 6, 10, 12, 13, 14, 17, 25, 33, 34, 66, 75, 81, 82, 85, 94, 131, 132, 143, 144 by Mayank Rawat.

ISBN: 978–81–317–3100–0

First Impression

Published by Dorling Kindersley (India) Pvt. Ltd.
Licensees of Pearson Education in South Asia.

Head Office: 7th Floor, Knowledge Boulevard, A-8 (A), Sector 62, Noida 201309, UP, India
Registered Office: 14 Local Shopping Centre, Panchsheel Park, New Delhi 110017, India

Typeset by Pen2Print Media Solutions Pvt. Ltd.

Printed in India by Chennai Micro Print

BRIEF CONTENTS

CONTENTS

CONTENTS

ABOUT THE AUTHORS

E. Suresh Kumar is Head, Department of English, University College of Engineering, Osmania University. He has visited several universities in the UK, the USA and the UAE on special invitations. He was the Principal Investigator of the Retraining Programme for the English lecturers in Andhra Pradesh, which was jointly conducted by the Directorate of Collegiate Education, Government of Andhra Pradesh and the Department of State, USA.

P. Sreehari is Academic Consultant in the Department of English, University College of Engineering, Osmania University. He has conducted several workshops and training programmes on soft skills, accent neutralization, communication skills and personality development in India and abroad.

J. Savithri teaches English at the Department of English, Osmania University. She specializes in English language teaching. She has authored a book and several research articles on English language teaching, with special reference to regional medium students.

PREFACE

Effective English attempts to teach communication skills in English in a way that is closely related to the acquisition of life skills. Each chapter begins with a passage for reading and is followed by comprehension, grammar, and thinking and writing exercises. The other three skills of listening, speaking and writing have been closely connected to issues like goal-setting, interpersonal communication, managing stress, presentation skills, and writing reports, resumes, and statements of purpose. We have also covered functional grammar, spelling, and pronunciation. The book contains exhaustive appendixes on grammar, common errors, and pronunciation.

We hope that this book will mark a new beginning for the teaching of language skills in India.

Acknowledgements

We would like to thank our family, our colleagues and the Pearson's editorial team, especially Ms Debjani Dutta and Mr Arani Banerjee.

1

In this unit

Reading
"A Hero" by R. K. Narayan

Structural Grammar
Adverbs

Listening
Tips for Personality Development

Speaking
Speaking About Personality Traits
Facing an Interview

Writing
Process of Writing
Writing on Role Models

Vocabulary
Words on Personality

Pronunciation
Word Stress
Stress and Grammatical Category

Functional Grammar
Question Tags

Spelling

Do you remember the first time you slept alone? It is one of the first steps towards growing up. It is all about conquering fear—the fear of darkness and loneliness. Read the following story about a child whose first attempt to sleep alone results in an incident that turns him into a 'hero'.

R. K. Narayan (1906–2001) was one of the greatest writers of Indian literature in English. He is best known for his stories and novels about Malgudi, a fictional town near Mysore. His novel, *Guide*, was made into a successful Hindi film.

Reading

"A Hero" by R. K. Narayan

For Swaminathan, events took an unexpected turn. Father looked over the newspaper he was reading under the hall lamp and said, "Swami, listen to this: 'News is to hand of the bravery of a village lad who, while returning home by the jungle path, came face to face with a tiger…'" The paragraph described the fight the boy had with the tiger and his flight up a tree, where he stayed of half a day till some people came that way and killed the tiger.

After reading it through, Father looked at Swaminathan fixedly and asked, "What do you say to that?"

Swaminathan said, "I think he must been a very strong and grown-up person, not at all a boy. How could a boy fight a tiger?"

"You think you are wiser than the newspaper?" Father **sneered**. "A man may have the strength of an elephant and yet be a **coward**: whereas another may have the strength of a straw, but if he has courage he can do anything. Courage is everything, strength and age are not important."

Swami said, "How can it be, Father? Suppose I have all the courage, what can I do if a tiger should attack me?"

"Leave alone strength, can you prove you have courage? Let me see if you can sleep alone tonight in my office room."

A **frightful** suggestion, Swaminathan thought. He had always slept beside his Granny, and any change in this arrangement kept him **trembling** and awake all night. He hoped at first that his father was only joking. He **mumbled** a weak "Yes" and tried to change the subject. He said very loudly and with a great deal of enthusiasm, "We are going to admit even elders in our cricket club hereafter. We are buying brand new bats and balls. Our captain has asked me to tell you …"

"We'll see about it later," Father cut in. "You must sleep alone hereafter." Swaminathan realized that the matter and gone beyond his control: from a challenge it had become a plain command; he knew his father's **tenacity** at such moments.

"From the first of next month I'll sleep alone, Father."

"No, you must do it now. It is **disgraceful** sleeping beside Granny or Mother like a baby. You are in the Second Form and I don't at all like the way you are being brought up," he said, and looked at his wife, who was rocking the **cradle**.

Swaminathan's father sat **gloomily** gazing at the newspaper on his lap. Swaminathan rose silently and tiptoed away to his bed in the passage. Granny was sitting up in her bed, and remarked, "Boy, are you already feeling sleepy? Don't you want a story?" Swaminathan made wild **gesticulations** to silence

sneered
laughed at

coward
a person who is too eager to avoid danger, difficulty or pain

frightful
causing fear

trembling
shaking with fear

mumbled
spoke quietly and in a way that was not clear

tenacity
the determination to continue what you are doing

disgraceful
very bad; shameless

cradle
a small bed for a baby, especially one that swings from side to side

gloomily
sadly and hopelessly

gesticulations
movements of the hands, arms or head, etc. to express an idea or feeling

whispered
spoke in a low voice

snored
breathed in a very noisy way while sleeping

groaned
made a deep, long sound showing pain and unhappiness

pleaded
requested earnestly

slunk
walked away

his Granny, but that good lady saw nothing. So Swaminathan threw himself on his bed and pulled the blanket over his face.

Granny said, "Don't cover your face. Are you really very sleepy?" Swaminathan leant over and **whispered**, "Please, please shut up, Granny. Don't talk to me, and don't let anyone call me even if the house is on fire. If I don't sleep at once I shall perhaps die—" He turned over, curled and **snored** under the blanket till he found his blanket pulled away.

Presently, Father came and stood over him. "Swami, get up," he said. Swaminathan stirred and **groaned** as if in sleep. Father said, "Get up, Swami." Granny **pleaded**, "Why do you disturb him?"

"Get up, Swami," he said for the third time, and Swaminathan got up. Father rolled up his bed, took it under his arm, and said, "Come with me." Swaminathan looked at his Granny, hesitated for a moment, and followed his father into the office room. On the way he threw a look of appeal at his mother and she said, "Why do you take him to the office room? He can sleep in the hall, I think."

"I don't think so," Father said, and Swaminathan **slunk** behind him with bowed head.

"Let me sleep in the hall, Father," he pleaded. "Your office room is very dusty and there may be scorpions behind your law books."

"There are no scorpions, little fellow. Sleep on the bench if you like."

"Can I have a lamp burning in the room?"

"No. You must learn not to be afraid of darkness. It is only a question of habit. You must cultivate good habits."

"Will you at least leave the door open?"

"All right. But promise you will not roll up your bed and go to your Granny's side at night. If you do it, mind you, I will make you the laughing stock of your school."

Swaminathan felt cut off from humanity. He was pained and angry. He didn't like the strain of cruelty he saw in his father's nature. He hated the newspaper for printing the tiger's story. He wished that the tiger hadn't spared the boy, who didn't appear to be a boy, after all, but a monster...

As the night advanced and the silence in the house deepened, his heart beat faster. He remembered all the stories of devils and ghosts he had heard in his life. He was faint with fear. A ray of light from the street lamp strayed in and cast shadows on the wall. Through the stillness, all kinds of noises reached his ears—the ticking of the clock, the rustle of trees, the sound of snoring, and some vague night insects humming. He covered himself so completely that he could hardly breathe. Every moment he expected the devils to come up to carry him away.

crouched
bent his knees and lowered himself

reassuring
comforting; encouraging

Swaminathan hurriedly got up and spread his bed under the bench and **crouched** there, it seemed to be a much safer place, more compact and **reassuring**. He shut his eyes tight and encased himself in his blanket once again and, unknown to himself, fell asleep, and dreamt that a tiger was chasing him. His feet stuck to the ground. He **desperately** tried to escape but his feet would not move; the tiger was at his back, and he could hear its claws scratch ground … scratch, scratch, and then a light thud … Swaminathan tried to open his eyes, but his eyelids would not open and the **nightmare** continued. It threatened to continue forever. Swaminathan groaned in despair.

With a desperate effort he opened his eyes. He put his hand out to feel his Granny's presence at his side, as was his habit, but he only touched the wooden leg of the bench. And his lonely state came back to him. He sweated with fright. And now what was this **rustling**? As it came nearer, he crawled out from under the bench, hugged it with all his might, and used his teeth on it like a mortal weapon…

desperate
anxious

nightmare
frightening experience or dream

rustling
the sound of leaves

"Aiyo! Something has bitten me," went forth an agonized, thundering cry and was followed by a heavy tumbling and falling amidst furniture. In a moment, Father, cook and a servant came in, carrying lights.

And all three of them fell on the burglar who lay amidst the furniture with a bleeding ankle…

Congratulations were showered on Swaminathan the next day. His classmates looked at him with respect and his teacher patted his back. The Headmaster said that he was a true scout. Swaminathan had bitten into the flesh of one of the most notorious housebreakers of the district and the police were grateful to him for it.

The Inspector said, "Why don't you join the police when you grow up?"

Swaminathan said for the sake of politeness, "Certainly, yes," though he had quite made up his mind to be an engine driver, a railway guard, or a bus conductor later in life.

When he returned home from the club that night, Father asked, "Where is the boy?"

"He is asleep."

"Already!"

"He didn't have a wink of sleep the whole of last night," said his mother.

"Where is he sleeping?"

"In his usual place," Mother said casually. "He went to bed at seven-thirty."

"Sleeping beside his Granny again!" Father said. "No wonder he wanted to be asleep before I could return home—clever boy!"

Mother lost her temper. "You let him sleep where he likes. You needn't risk his life again …" Father mumbled as he went in to change, "All right, **mollycoddle** and spoil him as much as you like. Only don't blame me afterwards …"

Swaminathan, following the whole conversation from under the blanket, felt tremendously **relieved** to hear that his father was giving up on him.

mollycoddle
pamper; overprotect

relieved
felt happy

Comprehension

1. Why did Swami's father read out the news item to Swami?
2. Why did Swami consider the village lad to be a monster?
3. Why did Swami's father force him to sleep alone?
4. Why couldn't Swami sleep peacefully even under the bench?
5. How did Swami become the hero after that sleepless night?

Think and Write

Remember that the courage that Swaminathan showed was accidental. The role of Swaminathan's father is that of a hard task-master. Teachers, parents, and elders often treat children either with reprimands or with blind affection. Both are extremes, and we need to avoid them. We must let children develop courage, gain success, and learn their lessons on their own and at their own pace. Narayan focuses on the innocence of childhood, the myths that the media create, and the pressures of adolescence as it sets in.

The narrative is simple and yet has an element of surprise. But, with characteristic irony and mild humour, Narayan provides depth to it. He refuses to make it a conventional story of changing fortune or coming-of-age, but makes it more realistic.

Write about the most frightening experience you have ever had.

Structural Grammar

Use the words from the box and complete the sentences.

desperately	gloomily	tremendously	hurriedly	completely

1. Swaminathan's father sat gloomily gazing at the newspaper on his lap.
2. He covered himself so ____________ that he could hardly breathe.
3. Swaminathan ____________ got up and spread his bed under the bench and crouched there.
4. He ____________ tried to escape but his feet would not move.
5. Swaminathan felt ____________ relieved to hear that his father was giving up on him.

The words you used in the above exercise were adverbs. While adjectives describe nouns, adverbs describe verbs, adjectives as well as other adverbs. Read the following sentence:

P. T. Usha ran *very fast* in the Moscow Olympics

Here, 'fast' is an adverb, as it qualifies the verb 'ran'. 'Very' is also an 'adverb', and qualifies 'fast'.

Listening

Tips for Personality Development

Listening Exercise 1

Listen to the talk in which a person talks about how to develop one's personality. Listen to the talk again and jot down important words and phrases as you hear about the following:

- Defining personality

____

____

____

- Factors that influence personality development

____

____

____

- Having a vision

- Imagining yourself becoming what you want to be

- Being clear about goals

- Being assertive

- Being mentally sound

- Being physically fit

- Being spiritually strong

- Building your confidence

- Communicating effectively

- Cultivating a sense of humour

- Dealing with people on a win-win basis

- Developing a sense of appreciation

- Developing critical thinking

- Developing your creativity

- Having a sense of gratitude

- Having self-esteem

- Having self-motivation

- Learning the ways to overcome failure

- Learning to deal with criticism

- Learning to empathize

- Managing your stress and anger well

- Maturing with age

- Never being complacent

- Thinking positively

- Valuing relationships

- Being a role model

Speaking

Talking About Personality Traits

Speaking Exercise 1

Given below are words that can be used to describe people in positive and negative ways.

Try using these words to describe yourself and your classmates.

affectionate	annoying	arrogant
boisterous	brave	bully
calm	caring	cunning
diffident	domineering	dynamic
easy-going	empathetic	enigmatic
fastidious	fickle	frugal
gentle	greedy	gullible
hardworking	heroic	hot-tempered
lazy	lively	loyal
magnanimous	manipulative	mawkish
obdurate	obnoxious	optimistic
pessimistic	petulant	picky
rebellious	resourceful	responsible
secretive	selfish	sensible
tenacious	timid	tyrant
understanding	unfeeling	unyielding
vengeful	visionary	vivacious
waspish	wicked	witty
youthful	yucky	yuppie
zealous	zestful	

*Shanti is an **affectionate** older sister.*

Speaking Exercise 2

Imagine that you are facing an interview. The questions that you are asked are given below. Make a pair and say the answers aloud. After you've done this, you can write the responses in the space assigned.

Interviewer: Good Morning, Harish. Was it difficult finding the way?

Harish:

Interviewer: I see that you've opted for history for your main examination even though you are an engineering student. Could you explain your choice?

Harish:

Interviewer: We do understand that you have a keen interest in the country's past but there is a feeling that people opt for history because it is easier to score high marks.

Harish:

Interviewer: What do you think is India's biggest problem?

Harish:

Interviewer: Was Gandhiji's political strategy to gain independence good enough? What is your opinion of his role in the Khilafat movement?

Harish:

Interviewer: How do you think the bureaucracy should react in the face of the current economic recession?

Harish:

Interviewer: How do you think the nuclear deal will help India's energy crisis?

Harish:

Interviewer: How many steps did you climb to reach our office?

Harish:

___

___

___

Interviewer: You come from a rather remote village. How did you manage to come this far?

Harish:

___

___

___

Interviewer: You seem to have done very badly in your matriculation. Why?

Harish:

___

___

___

Interviewer: That's all from us, Harish. Have a good day.

Which presentation strategies are the most effective during an interview?

1. It is best to maintain eye contact with the interviewer while wearing a smile. If you do not look at the person you are speaking to, this may be mistaken for dishonesty or a lack of confidence. Do not stare continuously either, or you will make the interviewer feel uncomfortable. A smile, if affable and friendly, covers up for any offence that the eye contact may cause.
2. Be honest about why you want to change your job. Whether it is money or job satisfaction, it is best to say as much. If you use vague words like 'job opportunity' and 'core competence' or 'growth', you end up compromising your ability to negotiate. Be candid, but not rude.
3. Sit in a relaxed way, but do not lean back on your chair or clasp your hands. Lean forward and appear keen on answering questions.
4. Needless to say, wish the interviewer(s) at the beginning of the interview and thank them at the end of it.
5. Do not appear too eager to get the job. Never get into ideological debates or polemics. You can never convince any one about any political issue within an hour, and you will only waste your own time.
6. Do not speak too fast.
7. Tackle tricky questions by not answering them directly. A question like 'How can you increase the market share of a product that has been off the shelf for twelve years?' is not asked because the marketing manager is looking for a brainwave from you. He wants to see if you can tackle a difficult query from a customer. The best answer in this case would be to ask for sales figures of the product prior to its discontinuation. And also ask for information about the competition. If the interviewer is not trying to deny you a chance just because he is biased against you, he will change the topic.

8. Be prepared for some bullying. People like to test your man-management skills. They might make politically incorrect comments. The best strategy is to show no tolerance for such behaviour. This also reduces the chances of workplace harassment.
9. Ask relevant questions. Do not talk of irrelevant things like cricket news or election results. You will lose time and will not be able to ask questions about the nature of your job, compensation, leave facilities, etc.
10. They might ask you about your family. Do not boast about the uncle who is a poet or the cousin who is a finance secretary. Stick to your immediate family and the bare facts. Do not reveal more than the basics. You do not need to tell them that your father doesn't like late nights.

Writing

Essay Writing

Writing is a process, and you should familiarize yourself with the different stages involved in composition. Writing a good paragraph or an essay involves some stages. You can use the acronym **TOWER** to recall the five steps involved in writing a paragraph or essay. **TOWER** stands for thinking, organizing, writing, editing and rewriting.

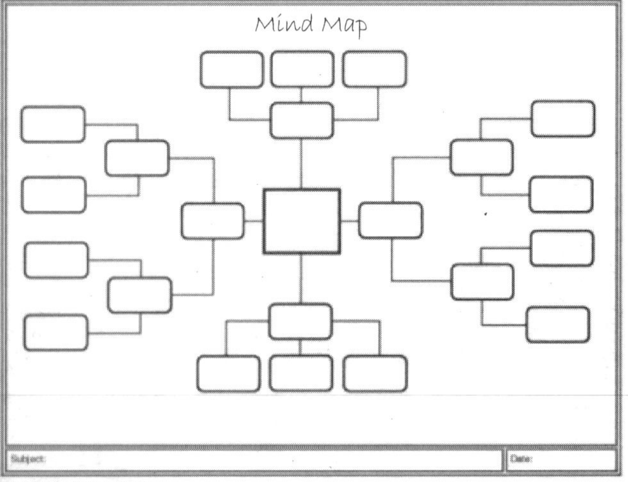

Thinking	Focus on key words and phrases related to your topic. Think about how much information ought to be included for each topic.
Organizing	Organize information using techniques like outlining, flow charts, grouping and mind mapping.
Writing	Write the first draft of the paragraph or essay.
Editing	Look for mistakes in language and in the arrangement of your ideas.
Rewriting	Correct all errors and write the final version.

A Sample Essay

Stage 1: Thinking/Brainstorming

The following key words were jotted down as the author thought about the topic.

architect of modern India   eminent engineer   simple vegetarian

teetotaller   hardworking   honest   statesman

visionary   Bharat Ratna

Stage 2: Organizing

The grouping technique was used to organize the information.

Personal	Achievements
simple	architect of modern India
vegetarian	eminent engineer
teetotaller	statesman
hardworking	visionary
honest	Bharat Ratna
lost his father at an early age	

Stage 3: Writing the First Draft

The following was the first draft:

Sir Mokshagundam visvesvaraya was an eminent engineer and statesman who played a key role in building of modern India. He received our country highest honour, the Bharat Ratna in 1955. He was responsible for building the very first electricity generation plant in Asia at Shivanasamudram near Mysore in 1894.

He had many acheivement to his credit these include implementing an extremely intricate system of irrigation in the Deccan area, designing and patenting a system of automatic weir water floodgates, and supervising the construction of the KRS dam across the Cauvery River from concept to inauguration.

The automatic flood gates designed were first installed in 1903 at the Khadakvasla reservoir near Pune. These gates were employed to rise the flood supply level of storage in the reservoir to the highest level likely to be attained by its flood without causing any damage to the dam. Based on the success of these gates, the same system was installed at the Tigra dam in Gwalior and the Krishnaraja Sagara (KRS) dam in Mysore.

Visvesvaraya achieved celebrity status when he designed a flood protection system to protect the city of Hyderabad floods. He was also instrumental in developing a system to protect Vishakapatnam port from sea erosion. Sir M. V. supervised the construction of the KRS dam across the Cauvery River from concept to inauguration. This dam created the biggest reservoir in Asia at the time it was built.

during his period of service with the Government of Mysore state, he was responsible for founding of under the aegis of that government the Mysore Soap Factory, the Parasitoid laboratory, the Bhadravati Iron & Steel Works, the SJ Polytechnic Institute, the Bangalore Agricultural University, the State Bank of Mysore, the Mandya Sugar Mills and numerous other industrial ventures. He also encouraged private investment in industry during his tenure as Diwan of Mysore.

Continued

Sir M. Visvesvaraya lead a very simple life. He was strict vegetarian and teetotaller. He was known for his honesty and integrity. In 1912, Maharaja of Mysore appointed Visvesvaraya as his Dewan. Before accepting the position of Dewan of Mysore, he invited all his relatives for dinner. He told them very clearly that he would accept the prestigious office on the condition that none of them would approach him for favours.

He known for sincerity, time management and dedication to a cause. He was also instrumental in charting out the plan for road construction between Tirumala and Tirupati.

Stage 4: Editing

Note the careless organization, spelling mistakes and incorrect grammar in the first draft.

Sir Mokshagundam ~~visvesvaraya~~ Visvesvaraya was an eminent engineer and statesman who played a key role in building of modern India. He received our ~~country~~country's highest honour, the Bharat Ratna, in 1955. He ~~was responsible for building the very first electricity generation plant in Asia at Shivanasamudram near Mysore in 1894.~~

~~He~~ had many ~~acheivement~~achievements to his credit ~~these.~~ These include implementing an extremely intricate system of irrigation in the Deccan ~~area~~, designing and patenting a system of automatic weir water floodgates, and supervising the construction of the Krishnaraja Sagara (KRS) dam across the Cauvery River from concept to inauguration. He was responsible for building the very first electricity generation plant in Asia at Shivanasamudram near Mysore in 1894. He was also instrumental in charting out the plan for road construction between Tirumala and Tirupati.

The automatic flood gates he designed were first installed in 1903 at the Khadakvasla reservoir near Pune. These gates were employed to ~~rise~~raise the flood supply level of storage in the reservoir to the highest level likely to be ~~attained~~reached by its flood without causing any damage to the dam. Based on the success of these gates, the same system was installed at the Tigra dam in Gwalior and the ~~Krishnaraja Sagara~~ (KRS) dam in Mysore.

~~Visvesvaraya~~ He achieved celebrity status when he designed a flood protection system to protect the city of Hyderabad from floods. He was also instrumental in developing a system to protect Vis~~h~~akhapatnam port from sea erosion. ~~Sir M. V. supervised the construction of the~~The KRS dam across the Cauvery Rriver ~~from concept to inauguration. This dam~~, constructed under his supervision, created ~~the biggest~~ a reservoir that was the biggest in Asia at ~~the~~ that time ~~it was built.~~

~~during~~During his period of service with the Government of Mysore state, under the aegis of that government he was responsible for founding ~~of under the aegis of that government~~ the Mysore Soap Factory, ~~the Parasitoida~~ parasitoid laboratory, the Bhadravati Iron & Steel Works, the S.J. Polytechnic Institute, the Bangalore Agricultural University, the State Bank of Mysore, the Mandya Sugar Mills and numerous other industrial ventures. He also encouraged private investment in industry during his tenure as ~~Diwan~~Dewan of Mysore.

~~Sir M.~~Mokshagundam Visvesvaraya ~~lead~~is an endearing figure not only for his public achievements but also for leading an exemplary personal life. He led a very simple life. He ~~was~~was a strict vegetarian and a teetotaller. ~~He~~, and was known for his honesty and integrity. In 1912, the Maharaja of Mysore appointed Visvesvaraya as his Dewan. Before accepting the position of Dewan of Mysore, he invited all his relatives for dinner. He told them very clearly that he would accept the prestigious office on the condition that none of them would approach him for favours.

~~He~~ He was also known for ~~sincerity,~~his time management and dedication to a cause. ~~He was also instrumental in charting out the plan for road construction between Tirumala and Tirupati.~~

Stage 5: Rewriting

Read the final version below, now free from all errors.

My Role Model: Mokshagundam Visvesvaraya

Sir Mokshagundam Visvesvaraya was an eminent engineer and statesman who played a key role in the building of modern India. He received our country's highest honour, the Bharat Ratna, in 1955. He had many achievements to his credit. These include implementing an extremely intricate system of irrigation in the Deccan, designing and patenting a system of automatic weir water floodgates, and supervising the construction of the Krishnaraja Sagara (KRS) dam across the Cauvery river from concept to inauguration. He was responsible for building the very first electricity generation plant in Asia at Shivanasamudram near Mysore in 1894. He was also instrumental in charting out the plan for road construction between Tirumala and Tirupati.

The automatic flood gates he designed were first installed in 1903 at the Khadakvasla reservoir near Pune. These gates were employed to raise the flood supply level of storage in the reservoir to the highest level likely to be reached by its flood without causing any damage to the dam. Based on the success of these gates, the same system was installed at the Tigra dam in Gwalior and the KRS dam in Mysore.

He achieved celebrity status when he designed a flood protection system to protect the city of Hyderabad from floods. He was also instrumental in developing a system to protect the Visakhapatnam port from sea erosion. The KRS dam across the Cauvery river, constructed under his supervision, created a reservoir that was the biggest in Asia at that time.

During his period of service with the Government of Mysore State, he was responsible for founding the Mysore Soap Factory, a parasitoid laboratory, the Bhadravati Iron & Steel Works, the S. J. Polytechnic Institute, the Bangalore Agricultural University, the State Bank of Mysore, the Mandya Sugar Mills and numerous other industrial ventures. He also encouraged private investment in industry during his tenure as Dewan of Mysore.

Mokshagundam Visvesvaraya is an endearing figure not only for his public achievements but also for leading an exemplary personal life. He led a very simple life. He was a strict vegetarian and a teetotaller, and was known for his honesty and integrity. In 1912, the Maharaja of Mysore appointed Visvesvaraya as his dewan. Before accepting the position of Dewan of Mysore, he invited all his relatives for dinner. He told them very clearly that he would accept the prestigious office on the condition that none of them would approach him for favours. He was also known for his time management and dedication to a cause.

Writing Exercise 1

Role models (people whom you admire) can set a standard for you to set your goals by. Write about your role model using the five-stage writing process shown here. Mention, among other things, the qualities and behaviour you like in your role model and which aspects of his/her personality you wish to emulate.

Writing Exercise 2

Writing from personal experience and knowledge of the world:

WHAT ARE WE?

We are human and inhuman

We are rational and irrational

We are creative and crazy

We are divine and infernal

We are sacred and sinful

We are daring and docile

We are selfless and selfish

We are sensible and senseless

We are sane and insane

We are sanguine and sanguinary

We are a bundle of endless contradictions.

Write your response to the above using your knowledge and experience of the world. Think specifically about what you hear, read and know about how people behave.

Vocabulary

Words That Describe Personalities

Use the given words and complete the sentences.

arrogant	boisterous	bully
diffident	domineering	empathetic
enigmatic	fastidious	gullible
mawkish	obnoxious	obdurate
petulant	picky	vengeful
visionary	waspish	yucky

1. Being empathetic by nature, Apurva was able to put herself in his shoes.
2. Arun finally turned ____________ because he was so badly humiliated by his colleagues.

3. Ashok thinks that he is smaller or less powerful than others. And he always lets others ____________ him into doing things he doesn't want to do.
4. Dr A. P. J. Abdul Kalam is known for his ____________ thinking.
5. Everyone was nervous because the boys were playing a ____________ game.
6. Karan makes cruel remarks. People think that he has a ____________ tongue.
7. Many quacks survive because there are people ____________ enough to believe them.
8. Movies that exaggerate emotions are termed ____________.
9. Mukesh is such an ____________ figure that no one can understand him completely.
10. Pavani thinks that her husband is ____________ because he never takes her feelings into consideration.
11. People think that Ganesh is ____________ because he gives too much attention to small details and wants everything to be correct and perfect.
12. Pinky is ____________ about her sarees.
13. Praveen's colleagues think that he is ____________ because he always complains in a childish way.
14. Sharmila felt very embarrassed, for she wore a ____________ grey dress.
15. Shekhar is unpleasantly proud and behaves as if he is more important than other people. Many find him ____________ and rude.
16. The president of the workers' union is ____________ about his demands. He refuses to change his mind even after so much pressure from the management.
17. Though Mamata does things really well, she is ____________ about her achievements. This gives the feeling that she is lacking in self-respect.
18. When Revathi is in a bad mood, she is ____________ to everyone.

Pronunciation

Word Stress

Listening Exercise 2

Listen to the words below and repeat them, making sure that part of the word in bold is more audible than the other parts.

1. affectionate
2. annoying
3. boisterous
4. cunning
5. domineering

6. dynamic
7. diffident
8. enigmatic
9. empathetic
10. gullible
11. magnanimous
12. manipulative
13. optimistic
14. pessimistic
15. visionary

Stress and Grammatical Categories

For most words in English, the grammatical category determines which part of the word is stressed. When words with two syllables are used as nouns or adjectives, the stress is on the first syllable, and when they are used as verbs, the stress is on the second syllable.

Listening Exercise 3

Listen to the words *rebel* and *convert* and note how stress shifts depending on the grammatical category of these words:

rebel (noun)	The **re**bels overthrew the dictator.
re**bel** (verb)	Rakesh re**bel**led against the system when he was very young.
convert (noun)	Smitha is a religious **con**vert.
con**vert** (verb)	She con**ver**ted herself recently.

Writing Exercise 3

Use the words below to write sentences as shown in this section. You can use a dictionary to find out the meanings of the words.

1. a) conflict (noun)

   ____

   ____

   ____

   b) conflict (verb)

   ____

   ____

   ____

2. a) content (noun)

____
____
____

b) content (verb)

____
____
____

3. a) contract (noun)

____
____
____

b) contract (verb)

____
____
____

4. a) convict (noun)

____
____
____

b) convict (verb)

____
____
____

5. a) decrease (noun)

____
____
____

b) decrease (verb)

____
____
____

6. a) desert (noun)

____
____
____

b) desert (verb)

____
____
____

7. a) discourse (noun)

____
____
____

b) discourse (verb)

8. a) escort (noun)

b) escort (verb)

9. a) exploit (noun)

b) exploit (verb)

10. a) export (noun)

b) export (verb)

11. a) extract (noun)

b) extract (verb)

12. a) import (noun)

b) import (verb)

13. a) insult (noun)

b) insult (verb)

14. a) object (noun)

b) object (verb)

15. a) perfume (noun)

b) perfume (verb)

16. a) permit (noun)

b) permit (verb)

17. a) present (noun)

b) present (verb)

18. a) refuse (noun)

b) refuse (verb)

____

____

____

19. a) reject (noun)

____

____

____

b) reject (verb)

____

____

____

20. a) survey (noun)

____

____

____

b) survey (verb)

____

____

____

Functional Grammar

Tag Questions

She is a great person, isn't she?

Question tag

In this sentence, a statement is followed by a mini-question. The whole sentence is a **tag question**, and the mini-question at the end is called a **question tag**.

We use tag questions at the end of statements to ask for confirmation.

The basic structure of tag questions is as follows:

+	–
Positive statement,	negative tag
You are an extrovert,	aren't you?
Negative statement,	positive tag
You are not an introvert,	are you?

Look at the following examples with positive statements:

1. You act first and then think, don't you?
2. We have learnt several ways of improving our personal effectiveness, haven't we?
3. He is good at juggling family and work, isn't he?
4. He should know what type of personality he is, shouldn't he?
5. Vinod has led an exemplary life, hasn't he?

Look at the following examples with negative statements:

1. Samatha isn't hard-working, is she?
2. Most of us are not goal-oriented, are we?
3. You don't use to-do lists, do you?
4. He hasn't got his priorities right, has he?
5. We won't buckle under pressure, will we?

Some special cases:

1. I am right, aren't I? **(not amn't I)**
2. He has many role models, doesn't he? **(not hasn't he)**
3. She has been successful in accomplishing her goals, hasn't she? **(not hasn't been she)**
4. Let's go, shall we? **(let's = let us)**
5. Give me a matchstick, will you? (**you** is absent in the positive negative statement.)

Question Tags with Imperatives

Sometimes, we use question tags with imperatives (invitations, orders and requests), but the sentence remains an imperative and does not require a direct answer. We use **won't** for invitations and requests. We use **can, can't, will, would** for orders.

imperative + question tag	note
1. Please join me for dinner, won't you?	request
2. Don't show it to her, will you?	order

Same-way Question Tags

You can sometimes use a positive-positive or negative-negative structure (same-way question tag) to express interest, surprise, anger, etc., and not to ask real questions.

positive + positive	note
1. So you're working on your project, are you? That's wonderful!	friendly
negative + negative	note
2. So you don't like my attitude, don't you?	unfriendly, angry

Notice that you can also use tag questions to ask for information or help, starting with a negative statement. This is a friendly or polite way of making a request.

Examples:

1. You wouldn't know where the post office is, would you?
2. You couldn't help me repair this machine, could you?

Answers to Tag Questions

You can often answer a tag question using **Yes** or **No**. Sometimes, you can answer by reversing the question tag.

Examples with correct answers:

1. You have a great personality, don't you? **Yes, I do.**
2. Swapna is not sentimental, is she? **Yes, she is.**
3. Ahmed can't express his ideas effectively, can he? **No, he can't.**

Intonation

You can change the meaning of a tag question with the pitch of your voice. With rising intonation, it sounds like a real question. But if your intonation falls, it sounds more like a statement that doesn't require a real answer.

Examples:

1. You don't know who I am, do you? (/ **rising)** real question
2. You don't know who I am, do you? (\ **falling)** statement

Writing Exercise 4

1. Complete the tag questions by matching the statements under A with question tags under B.

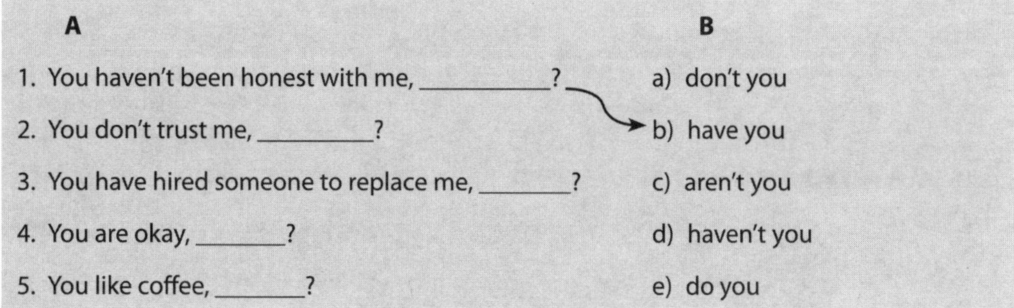

A	B
1. You haven't been honest with me, ________?	a) don't you
2. You don't trust me, ________?	b) have you
3. You have hired someone to replace me, ________?	c) aren't you
4. You are okay, ________?	d) haven't you
5. You like coffee, ________?	e) do you

2. With a partner, create a conversation that begins with one of the tag questions above. Decide who the characters are, and figure out what the situation is. Create and practise a role-playing scenario, and then present it to the class.

3. Use appropriate question tags and complete the following:

1. I drafted my report really well, __didn't I__?
2. Saritha seems to be good at multi-tasking, ____________?
3. Our boss is in a great mood today, ____________?
4. We mustn't tell her, ____________?
5. You have to go, ____________?

Spelling

Look at the sets of words below and circle the word with the correct spelling. Check your answers with the other members of your team. If you need to, use a good dictionary to find the correct spelling.

1.	boistarous	boisteros	bosterous	boisterous
2.	charecteristic	charactaristic	characteristic	charracteristic
3.	diffident	diffedent	diffidant	difident
4.	inttellectual	intelectual	intellectual	intallectual
5.	persanality	parsonality	personnality	personality
6.	posess	posses	possess	passess
7.	repet	ripeat	repeat	repeate
8.	senguinary	sanginary	sanguinery	sanguinary
9.	tetotaller	teetotaller	teetoteler	teetotallar
10.	visionary	visionery	visinary	visonary

2

Marine Ecosystems

In this unit

Reading
Marine Ecosystems
Structural Grammar
Clauses
Listening
Speeches on Capital Punishment
Euthanasia
Speaking
Distinguishing Between Fact and Opinion
Writing
Writing a Critical Essay
Structure of a Critical Essay
Vocabulary
Words That Describe Critical Thinking
Pronunciation
Intonation
Functional Grammar
Connectives or Transition Devices
Spelling

Concern for preserving our environment is often limited to planting trees, cleaning up waste, and controlling fuel emission. The world of the marine ecosystem is unknown to most of us. We need to preserve underwater life, not only for its beauty and diversity, but also because this fragile ecosystem nurtures our food supply and controls the temperatures of the world. Read the following piece to know more.

Reading

Marine Ecosystems

Marine **ecosystems** are a part of the **aquatic** system, the largest on the planet, covering over 70 per cent of the Earth's surface. The habitats that make up this vast system range from the productive nearshore regions to the barren ocean floor. Important marine ecosystems include oceans, estuaries and salt marshes, coral reefs and other tropical communities like mangrove forests, and coastal areas like lagoons, kelp and sea-grass beds and inter-tidal systems.

Marine ecosystems are home to a host of different species, ranging from tiny planktonic organisms that comprise the base of the marine food web to large marine **mammals** like whales. Birds are also plentiful, including shorebirds, gulls, wading birds and terns. Therefore, many animal species rely on marine ecosystems for both food and shelter from **predators**.

Marine ecosystems contain several **unique** qualities that set them apart from other aquatic ecosystems, the key factor being the presence of dissolved compounds in seawater, especially salts. The total gram weight of dissolved substances (salts) in one kilogram of seawater is referred to as salinity. In general, 85 per cent of the dissolved substances in seawater are sodium (Na) and chlorine (Cl). On average, seawater has a salinity of 35 parts per thousand grams (ppt) of water. These dissolved compounds give seawater its distinctive 'salty' taste, affect the species composition of particular marine **habitats**, and prevent oceans from freezing during the winter. Daily changes in factors such as weather, currents, and seasons as well as variations in climate and location will cause salinity levels to vary among different marine ecosystems.

In areas such as estuaries, tidal marshes and mangrove forests, tidal and freshwater influences from river and streams makes it necessary for marine organisms to adapt to a wide range of salinity levels. These organisms, including mussels, clams and barnacles, are called euryhaline (salt tolerant) organisms. Other organisms are unable to tolerate such changes in salinity. These organisms are considered to be stenohaline (salt intolerant). These species require more constant levels of salinity, forcing them to either migrate to new areas when fluctuations in salinity levels occur or areas where salinity change is minimal (e.g., the deep ocean).

Like other aquatic ecosystems, marine ecosystems require nutrients and light to produce food and energy. However, both nutrients and light are limiting factors in marine ecosystem productivity. Like many other aquatic plants, photosynthetic marine organisms (i.e., phytoplankton) rely upon sunlight and **chlorophyll** to absorb visible light from the sun as well as nitrogen, phosphorus, and silicon to generate food and promote growth and reproduction. However, the amount of light penetrating the ocean surface tends to decrease with increasing water depth, and thus photosynthesis can only take place within a small band near the surface of the water called the photic zone.

ecosystem
the relationship between living creatures and their environment

aquatic
relating to water

mammal
a warm-blooded animal that gives birth to offspring and produces milk

predator
an animal that kills and eats other animals

unique
unusual or special

In addition, nutrient availability often varies significantly from place to place. For example, in the open ocean, nutrient levels are often very poor, causing primary production to be very low. In contrast, nearshore waters such as estuaries and marshes are often rich in nutrients, allowing primary production to be very high. In some instances, nearshore ecosystems have an excess of nutrients due to runoff and other **terrestrial** sources. Excess nutrients can cause an over-stimulation of primary production, depleting oxygen levels in coastal habitats.

Marine ecosystems are very important to the overall health of both marine and terrestrial environments. According to the World Resources Center, coastal habitats alone account for approximately a third of all marine biological productivity, and estuarine ecosystems (i.e., salt marshes, seagrasses and mangrove forests) are among the most productive regions on the planet. In addition, other marine ecosystems such as coral reefs provide food and shelter to the highest levels of marine diversity in the world.

The diversity and productivity of marine ecosystems are also important to human survival and well-being. These habitats provide us with a rich source of food and income, and support species that serve as animal feed, fertilizers for crops, additives in foods and cosmetics. Areas such as mangroves, reefs, and seagrass beds also provide protection to coastlines by reducing wave action, and helping to prevent **erosion**, while areas such as salt marshes and estuaries have acted as sediment sinks, filtering runoff from the land. Despite the importance of marine ecosystems, increased human activities such as overfishing, coastal development, pollution, and the introduction of exotic species have caused significant damage and pose a serious threat to marine biodiversity.

habitat
natural environment in which animals or plants live

chlorophyll
a green substance in plants through which plants manufacture food with the help of sunlight

terrestrial
relating to the earth

erosion
a condition where the surface of the earth gradually gets destroyed by the forces of nature

Comprehension

1. What are the important marine ecosystems?
2. Which species comprise the marine food web?
3. What is the importance of salinity?
4. What are the limiting factors in marine ecosystems in terms of manufacturing food?
5. Why are marine ecosystems very important?

Structural Grammar

Clauses

A clause is a meaningful group of words that has a subject and a predicate. A 'subject' of a sentence is the answer that you get when you ask a sentence, 'Who is it about?' The predicate is the answer that you get when you ask, 'Well, what does the sentence have to say about its subject?'

The part of a sentence that does not depend on any other part for its meaning is called a *main clause*.

A *subordinate clause* is the part that qualifies that clause, explaining its nature and quality, showing relationships, establishing its cause and effect, or contrast, or behaves as a subject or object of the sentence.

Remember:

An *adjective clause* acts like an adjective in a sentence.

An *adverb clause* establishes comparison, cause and effect, relationship of time, and condition.

A *noun clause* behaves as a noun; it is often the subject or the object of the sentence.

In the following sentence, identify the **main** and **subordinate** clauses:

1. Some species require more constant levels of salinity, forcing them to either migrate to new areas when fluctuations in salinity levels occur, or to seek out areas where salinity change is minimal.
2. Marine ecosystems are very important to the overall health of both marine and terrestrial environments.
3. Marine ecosystems contain several unique qualities that set them apart from other aquatic ecosystems, the key factor being the presence of dissolved compounds in seawater, especially salts.
4. In the open ocean, nutrient levels are often very poor, causing primary production to be low.

Think and Write

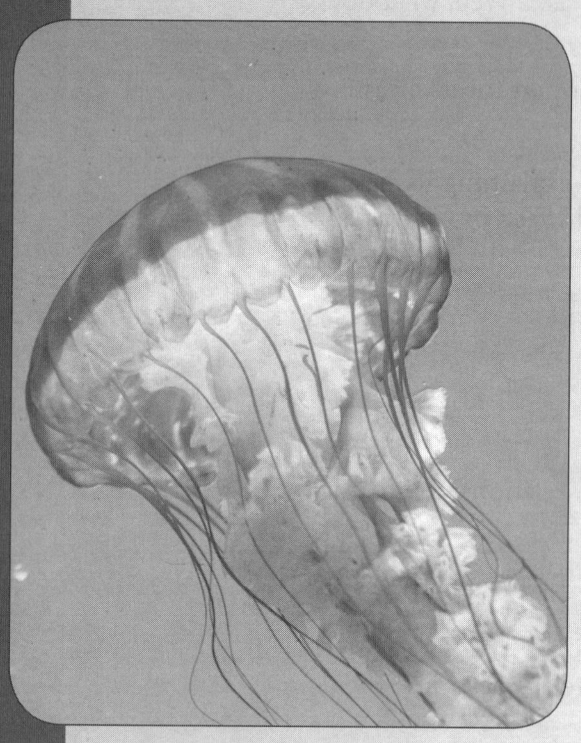

Writing on important issues such as the environment means employing statistics, descriptive sentences and persuasion. The above passage is written in a style that presents information with lucidity and directness. The use of the active voice, careful placing of adjectives and a neat structure makes the writing effective. You can also use bullet points, but do so with caution. They tend to destroy the flow of the text.

Write an article on an issue that you feel is important.

Listening

Speeches on Capital Punishment

Listening Exercise 1

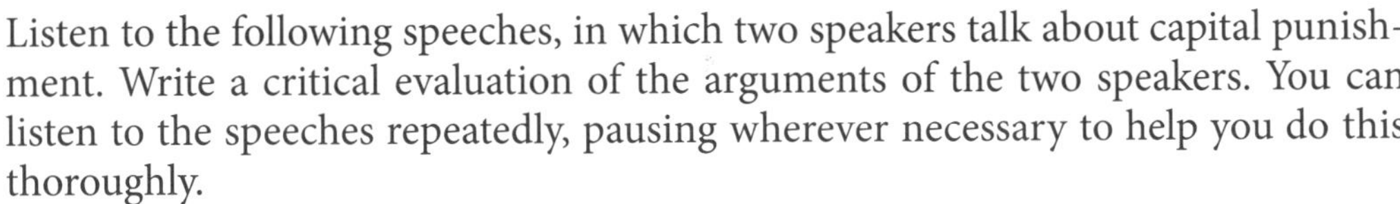

Listen to the following speeches, in which two speakers talk about capital punishment. Write a critical evaluation of the arguments of the two speakers. You can listen to the speeches repeatedly, pausing wherever necessary to help you do this thoroughly.

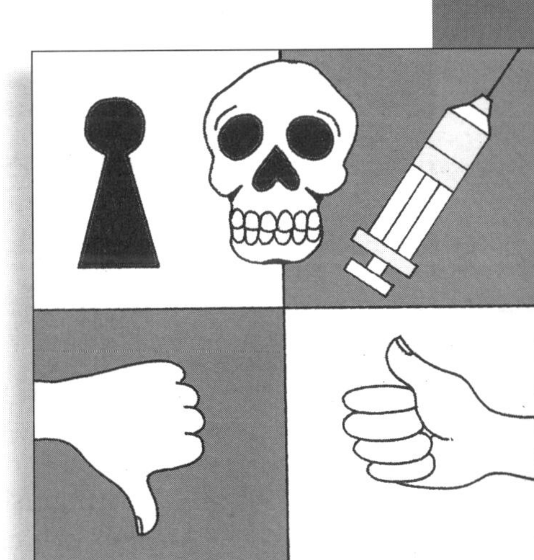

Evaluation of the arguments of speaker 1

____

____

____

Evaluation of arguments of speaker 2

____

____

____

Group Discussion on Euthanasia

Group Discussion Techniques

- Introduce yourself as briefly and as precisely as possible. Do not say that you topped your college exams. Do not attract competition; you don't need any.
- State the problem to be discussed. Avoid responding to an angry or provocative statement by a fellow participant. Try to understand the reason behind the provocation. Avoid attacking the participant's position directly, but suggest a solution or compromise. Refutation should be a part of your argument, but you should not waste time by refuting outright prejudices.
- Do not monopolize the discussion. Let everyone speak. Remember that you are evaluated on your *individual* efforts as a part of a larger group.
- Refer to all participants by name. Achieve a degree of first-name familiarity.
- As you carry out the discussion, try to emerge as the leader. You can do that by be a facilitator. Provide leads or prompts to your fellow participants, summarize and conclude on solutions discussed and offer out-of-the-box but practicable ideas. Do not, however, be overassertive, or the other participants will resent your input.

Listening Exercise 2

Listen to the following group discussion on euthanasia, and then write a critical analysis of the group discussion. As in the previous exercise, you can listen to the discussion repeatedly.

Analysis of the group discussion on euthanasia

____

____

____

Speaking

Pair/Group Work: Distinguishing Between Fact and Opinion

Distinguishing between a fact and an opinion is an important aspect of improving one's critical thinking. A fact is a statement that can be proven true or verified by observation, research, and/or experiment. An opinion expresses one's belief, feeling, view, idea, or judgement about something or someone.

Discuss the following and decide if they are fact or opinion:

1. Every human activity is latently political.
2. Politics is an integral part of human civilization.
3. We are far better off than our ancestors were.
4. Valentine's Day celebrations lead to consumerism amongst our youth.
5. Valentine's Day is celebrated in most parts of the world.
6. A survey conducted among patients at a cancer hospital revealed that over 75 per cent of those affected by the disease in their lungs were smokers.
7. The Taj Mahal is one of the new seven wonders of the world.
8. The Taj Mahal is perhaps the most magnificent of new seven wonders of the world.
9. Intellectual apathy is the root cause of social unrest.
10. Barking dogs seldom bite.

Speaking Exercise 1

Imagine that you are a customer trying to buy shirts. The salesman's cues are given; speak out the responses that you are likely to make in such a situation.

Salesperson: Good evening, sir. How may I help you?

You: ______________________________

Salesman: What is your budget?

You: ______________________________

Salesman: Here is the range that you can choose from.

You: ______________________________

Salesman: Sir, all of our goods are imported from Malayasia.

You: ______________________________

Salesman: Thank you, sir. Please go to the billing counter and I'll have the shirts sent. Have a nice day, and do visit us again soon.

You: ______________________________

Writing

Writing a Critical Essay

A critical essay is a coherent and logically developed presentation of a thesis or central idea, which should be clear and specific. The thesis must be supported with sufficient evidence and careful argument to convince the reader of its importance and validity. Although each writer's composing process is unique, the narrowing, organizing and shaping of an essay often takes place in the initial stages of the process.

Sethu, an undergraduate student, had to write an essay on the Harry Potter books. He wanted to see if the plots of the Harry Potter books were similar to detective fiction. Here are the steps he followed in writing the essay.

Steps in Writing a Critical Essay

Step 1: Research	Research the selected topic, gathering information from various sources.
Step 2: Evaluate	Critically evaluate the information. Assess the material in terms of structure and ideas, as well as the way these ideas refer to the topic. At this point, ask yourself whether the material is sufficient, and whether the viewpoints are reasonable.

Step 3: Identify the scope	Narrow down the scope of your topic and decide on the thesis statement for your essay. You should be able to formulate this thesis in a single sentence or two. Ask yourself: **What exactly is the point that I want the reader to understand?**
Step 4: Analyse and review	Analyse your material and review it until you are familiar enough with it to form a judgement or take a position on the topic selected. Organize your information in light of this argument or thesis.
Step 5: Arrange your arguments	Divide the material you have gathered into the separate points of the argument and arrange these in order of increasing strength, ending with your most convincing point. Deal with opposite points of view. Disposing—in a fair and logical manner—of counter-arguments in the body of your essay strengthens your thesis.
Step 6: Prepare outline	Prepare a detailed outline or plan before writing the first draft. As you do so, check that there are no contradictions in your argument, no gaps in your reasoning and no irrelevant points.
Step 7: Write the first draft	Write the first draft based on an appropriate structure and then check it for errors.
Step 8: Write the final text	Write or type the final, error-free version.

The Structure of a Critical Essay

Read this critical essay and note its structure:

Harry Potter as Detective

Title: *Your title should reflect the thesis or central argument of your essay.*

1. What makes Harry Potter popular? One answer might be that the books belong to the genre of detective fiction. In this essay, I explore the many features the Harry Potter books share with detective fiction.

1. Introduction: *The first paragraph of your essay serves as the introduction. It introduces the main idea of your essay. In the introduction, you should capture the interest of your reader and explain why your topic or argument is important. You must include your thesis statement and provide some background information about your topic. You may offer an overview of your essay without giving a full summary of what is to follow.*

2. Within the category of detective fiction, the Harry Potter books use elements from two sub-categories: the 'whodunit' and the 'thriller'. The 'whodunit' involves the investigation of crimes that have been committed before the actual action of the plot begins, while the 'thriller' consists of new adventures that take place as the action progresses.

3. Each book in the Harry Potter series begins with a particular mystery and ends with its resolution, brought about by Harry and his friends. Though each book repeats this formula, it also takes off from where the previous one ended, thereby tying up the individual mysteries into a larger, continuous adventure. It is this presence of a repetitive formula within an overarching narrative that is the hallmark of serial fiction, and the Harry Potter books resemble the Superman or the Batman series in this respect. As Harry and his friends unravel one mystery after another, they also move progressively closer to the final adventure of a direct confrontation with their arch-enemy, Voldemort.

2–3. Body or supporting paragraphs: Supporting paragraphs develop the main idea of your essay and make up the main body of your essay. Each paragraph should have a major point, supporting points, and a summary. The paragraph must be related logically to the preceding and following ones. Use connecting words such as 'however', 'therefore', 'in addition to' and 'nevertheless' (refer to the grammar section of this unit to study them at length) to ensure smooth and clear transitions between points and paragraphs. Make sure that the argument progresses in a manner that is both coherent and convincing.

4. The Harry Potter books use the plot structure of the 'suspense novel' in order to create and sustain anticipation in the readers about the next instalment of the series. Harry emerges as a hero not only because he risks his life repeatedly to resolve mysteries, but also because he ultimately decides to face (and thereby overcomes) death in his pursuit of truth and justice. Thus, the Harry Potter books draw upon the conventions of serial detective fiction in which there is a final victory of the 'detective hero'—a victory that reveals the truth behind the puzzles he faces and signals the ultimate moral conquest of goodness over evil.

4. Conclusion or Summary Paragraph: The summary paragraph comes at the end of your essay, after you have finished developing your ideas. The summary paragraph is often called a conclusion. It summarizes or restates the main idea of the essay. Restate the strongest points of your essay that support your main idea. Conclude your essay by restating the main idea in different words. Leave the reader with a sense that your essay is complete. Give general implications of your argument or suggest a plan for action.

Writing Exercise 2

Corporal punishment is a deliberate form of inflicting punishment with a view to disciplining or changing behaviour. Corporal punishment is still being practised in many parts of the world. Write a critical essay on corporal punishment.

Vocabulary

Words That Describe Critical Thinking

Study the meanings of the following words:

1.	logical	seeming reasonable or sensible
2.	fallacious	based on false ideas
3.	dogmatic	relating to a dogma or code of beliefs; stating one's opinions in a forceful manner
4.	controversial	causing a lot of disagreement
5.	premise	basis
6.	proposition	idea; suggestion
7.	critical	giving opinions using sound reasoning
8.	sentimental	influenced by emotional feelings
9.	objective	based on real facts and not influenced by personal beliefs or feelings
10.	subjective	based on personal beliefs or feelings, rather than on facts

Use the words given earlier and complete the following sentences:

1. He started his article with the premise that human relations are very complex in nature.
2. You must stay calm even when you are talking on a topic which is ___________ in nature.
3. You sound incredible if your arguments are _____________.
4. I've put my ___________ to the principal of the college for his consideration.
5. She gave a ________ account on the happenings in the office.
6. He made sure that his ideas were expressed in a ___________ way.
7. As he was very ___________ his ideas were not accepted by the majority.
8. It's a not an expensive wrist watch but it has great _________ value for me.
9. I can't really be __________ when I'm judging my best friend's work.
10. I think you are the most decisive person in the world, but I realize my judgement is rather ________________.

Pronunciation

Intonation

Intonation is an important aspect of pronunciation in English. Intonation refers to the rise and fall of pitch while speaking. Unlike stress, it does not distinguish words as nouns and verbs, but often conveys a range of meanings, emotions or situations.

Intonation performs an accentual function in that it enables speakers to make any part of their utterance prominent in accordance with the meaning they would convey.

A variety of meanings can be conveyed through intonation changes in a single sentence. Consider the sentence below in which you can stress each word in turn, and see the totally different meanings that come out.

His arguments are fallacious.

His **arguments** are fallacious.

His arguments **are** fallacious.

His arguments are **fallacious**.

Once you are clear on the intonation changes in these sentences, you can indicate the context to clarify the meaning:

His arguments are fallacious, not yours.

His **arguments** are fallacious, not his beliefs.

His arguments **are** fallacious, but they weren't always so.

His arguments are **fallacious**, not subjective.

Listening Exercise 3

1. Listen to and repeat the sentences below. Say the words in bold more audibly.

   She argued logically.

   She **argued** logically.

   She argued **logically**.

Now, add context words to clarify the meaning.

She argued logically, but her friend did not.

She **argued** logically, __________.

She argued **logically**, __________.

2. Listen to and repeat the sentences below. Say the part in bold more audibly.

   They noticed many logical fallacies in his speech.

   They **noticed** many logical fallacies in his speech.

   They noticed **many** logical fallacies in his speech.

   They noticed many **logical** fallacies in his speech.

   They noticed many logical **fallacies** in his speech.

   They noticed many logical fallacies in **his** speech.

   They noticed many logical fallacies in his **speech**.

Now, add context words to clarify the meaning.

They noticed many logical fallacies in his speech, ______________________________.

They noticed many logical fallacies in his speech, ______________________________.

They noticed many logical fallacies in his speech, ______________________________.

They noticed many logical fallacies in his speech, ______________________________.

They noticed many logical fallacies in his speech, ______________________________.

They noticed many logical fallacies in his speech, ______________________________.

They noticed many logical fallacies in his speech, ______________________________.

Functional Grammar

Connectives or Transition Devices

The first step in deciding whether something that you read or hear is an argument is to determine whether it has a conclusion, and if so, what that conclusion is. Once you identify the conclusion, you can usually figure out what the premises are. Identifying premises and conclusions based on the occurrence of *indicator words* works well in most cases. But there are exceptions. Some arguments often do not contain any indicator words at all. When this happens, ask yourself: what is the other person trying to get me to believe? Once you figure this out, you'll have the conclusion, and then it should be relatively easy to locate the premises.

Indicator Words or Connectives

Conclusion indicators include 'therefore', 'thus', 'so', 'hence', 'consequently', 'accordingly', 'entails that', 'implies that', 'we may conclude that', 'this establishes that', 'this gives us reason to suppose that' and 'in short'.

Premise indicators include 'because', 'for', 'since', 'after all', 'in as much as', 'in view of the fact that', 'in virtue of' and 'here are the reasons'.

A List of Connectives

The table presents some of the main connectives, classified roughly according to their broad meaning:

Broad Meaning	Connectives
addition	also; too; similarly; in addition; even; indeed; let alone
opposition	however; nevertheless; on the other hand; in contrast; though; alternatively; anyway; yet; in fact; even so
reinforcing	besides; anyway; after all

explaining	for example; for instance; in other words; that is to say; i.e.; e.g.
listing	first(ly) ... second(ly)...; first of all; finally; lastly; for one thing ... for another; in the first place; to begin with; next
indicating result	therefore; consequently; as a result; so; then
indicating time	then; meanwhile; later; afterwards; before (that); since (then); meanwhile

Meanings of Connectives with Examples

1. **accordingly:** in a way that is suitable or right for the situation

   She's an expert in this field, and is paid accordingly.

2. **alternatively:** used to suggest another possibility

   We could go out and eat or, alternatively, we could skip our meal.

3. **as well:** in addition; also

   Standing behind the lectern, he looked at the audience and decided he should wait for the rest to arrive, as well.

4. **as well:** to the same effect

   You might as well walk as drive in this traffic.

5. **because:** for the reason that

   We shouldn't buy this product because it doesn't appear to be genuine.

6. **because of:** as a result of

   The match was abandoned because of bad weather.

7. **besides:** in addition to; also

   You must collect information carefully—besides, you need to relate it to your topic.

8. **by far:** by a great amount

   Shashank is by far the best orator in the class.

9. **consequently:** as a result

   He didn't argue cogently and consequently didn't leave much impact on the audience.

10. **hence:** that is the reason or explanation for

    His father is a communist, hence his name—Stalin.

11. **however:** despite this

    This is one possible solution to the problem. However, there are others.

12. **inasmuch as:** used to introduce a phrase which explains why or how much something described in another part of the sentence is true

    Inasmuch as you are the boss, you are responsible for increasing the productivity of your organization.

13. **insofar as:** to the extent or degree that

    I agree only insofar as the style of presentation is concerned.

14. **likewise:** in the same way

    Just use these points for enhancing your critical thinking, and likewise to develop problem-solving skills.

15. **meanwhile:** until something expected happens

    Suman is expected to give a presentation next week. Meanwhile, he has to prepare for the same.

16. **meanwhile:** while something else is happening

    You'll be able to meet the principal after 10 minutes. Meanwhile, you may go through today's newspapers.

17. **moreover:** also and more importantly

    The whole speech is badly delivered. Moreover, the ideas are illogical.

18. **nevertheless or nonetheless:** despite what has just been said or referred to

    I watched this movie already, but I'd like to go with you again nevertheless.

19. **on the one hand ... on the other hand:** used when you are comparing two different facts or two opposite ways of thinking about a situation

    On the one hand I like playing cricket, but on the other hand I think it's a waste of time.

20. **therefore:** for that reason

    We were not convinced with her arguments therefore we did not give her a good grade.

21. **whereas:** compared with the fact that; but

    He normally analyses the issues objectively, whereas he's being very subjective this time.

22. **yet:** still; until the present time

    I haven't finished my report yet.

Complete the short passage below using the connectives given.

and *because* *besides* *just* *yet*

We shouldn't buy that new building set for our child ___________ he hasn't learned to take care of the toys he already has. ___________ yesterday he shoved all his toys into the closet and kicked them under his bed. ___________, I don't think he's old enough ___________ for that set. The box says it's for 8- to 10-year-olds, ___________ our child is only 4.

Complete the following sentences using the connectives given below:

although because because of but despite
even when ever since hence however moreover

1. Global meltdown has affected many sectors. However, the pharmaceutical industry is an exception.
2. Stress levels have increased __________ modern life has become much too complex.
3. Organizations will select you only if your resume is attractive. _________, it is a good idea to undergo some training in soft skills and personal grooming.
4. ____________ traffic chaos, commuting has become a nightmare in cities.
5. Prices of essential commodities continue to skyrocket ___________ zero inflation.
6. _____________ there are strict directives against corporal punishment, it continues to be widely practised in Indian schools.
7. We shouldn't hate politics because politics is an integral part of human civilization. _________, our lives are directly governed by policies framed by our politicians.
8. They were hoping to sell their car for Rs 2 lakhs, ________ settled for Rs 1.5 lakhs.
9. He went on lecturing ________________ the audience was restless.
10. He's been depressed ____________ he lost his job.

Spelling

Look at the sets of words below and circle the word with the correct spelling. Check your answers with the other members of your team. If you need to, use a good dictionary to find the correct spelling.

1.	controversil	contraversial	controversial	cantroversial
2.	erroneous	erraneous	eroneous	erroneus
3.	doclrinire	doctrinire	dactrinaire	doctrinaire
4.	falacious	fallacious	fellacious	fallecious
5.	appropriate	apropriate	approprite	appropriat
6.	euthenasia	ethanasia	euthanesia	euthanasia
7.	belief	beleif	bellief	belif
8.	intelectual	intallectual	intellectal	intellectual
9.	oppourtunity	oportunity	opportunity	opporttunity
10.	varriety	vareity	variety	veriety

3 The Verger

In this unit

Reading
"The Verger" by W. Somerset Maugham
Structural Grammar
Adjectives
Listening
Tips for Goal-Setting
Talking About Goals
Speaking
"What I Wish to Do"
Giving a Speech
Writing
Writing a Feature Story
Vocabulary
Synonyms
Collocations
Pronunciation
Word Stress
Syllables
Functional Grammar
Conditional Clauses
Wish Clauses
Spelling

We often choose our vocation simply to earn a livelihood. Rarely do we get a chance to do what we like and be paid for it. But even financial security may not compensate for missed opportunities. The following story is about a simple church official who becomes an entrepreneur. Does he regret his fortunes? To know more, read on.

William Somerset Maugham (1874–1965) was a British writer and was probably the highest paid author of his time. His magnum opus, *Of Human Bondage,* is considered to be one of the greatest coming-of-age novels of all times. His other novels include *Moon and Sixpence* and *Razor's Edge*.

Reading

"The Verger" by W. Somerset Maugham

There had been a christening that afternoon at St. Peter's, Neville Square, and Albert Edward Foreman still wore his **verger's** gown. He kept his new one, its folds as full and stiff as though it were made not of alpaca but of **perennial** bronze, for funerals and weddings (St. Peter's, Neville Square, was a church much favoured by the fashionable for these ceremonies) and now he wore only his second-best. He wore it with complacence for it was the dignified symbol of his office, and without it (when he took it off to go home) he had the disconcerting sensation of being somewhat insufficiently **clad**. He took pains with it; he pressed it and ironed it himself. During the sixteen years he had been verger of this church he had had a succession of such gowns, but he had never been able to throw them away when they were worn out and the complete series, neatly wrapped up in brown paper, lay in the bottom drawers of the wardrobe in his bedroom.

The verger busied himself quietly, replacing the painted wooden cover on the marble font, taking away a chair that had been brought for an infirm old lady, and waited for the **vicar** to have finished in the **vestry** so that he could tidy up in there and go home. Presently he saw him walk across the chancel, genuflect in front of the high altar and come down the aisle; but he still wore his **cassock**.

"What's he 'anging about for?" the verger said to himself "Don't 'e know I want my tea?"

The vicar had been but recently appointed, a red-faced energetic man in the early forties, and Albert Edward still regretted his predecessor, a **clergyman** of the old school who preached leisurely sermons in a silvery voice and dined out a great deal with his more aristocratic parishioners. He liked things in church to be just so, but he never fussed; he was not like this new man who wanted to have his finger in every pie. But Albert Edward was tolerant. St. Peter's was in a very good neighbourhood and the parishioners were a very nice class of people. The new vicar had come from the East End and he couldn't be expected to fall in all at once with the discreet ways of his fashionable congregation.

"All this 'ustle," said Albert Edward. "But give 'im time, he'll learn."

When the vicar had walked down the aisle so far that he could address the verger without raising his voice more than was becoming in a place of worship he stopped.

"Foreman, will you come into the vestry for a minute. I have something to say to you."

"Very good, sir."

The vicar waited for him to come up and they walked up the church together.

verger
an official in a church who takes care of the interior of a church and performs church ceremonies

perennial
permanent; recurring

clad
dressed

vicar
a kind of priest

vestry
a room in a church

cassock
a long, loose, usually black piece of clothing worn especially by priests

"A very nice christening, I thought sir. Funny 'ow the baby stopped cryin' the moment you took him."

"I've noticed they very often do," said the vicar, with a little smile. "After all I've had a good deal of practice with them."

It was a source of subdued pride to him that he could nearly always quiet a whimpering infant by the manner in which he held it and he was not unconscious of the amused admiration with which mothers and nurses watched him settle the baby in the crook of his surpliced arm. The verger knew that it pleased him to be complimented on his talent.

clergyman
a person ordained for religious service

trifle
little

The vicar preceded Albert Edward into the vestry. Albert Edward was a **trifle** surprised to find the two churchwardens there. He had not seen them come in. They gave him pleasant nods.

"Good afternoon, my lord. Good afternoon, sir," he said to one after the other.

They were elderly men, both of them and they had been churchwardens almost as long as Albert Edward had been verger. They were sitting now at a handsome refectory table that the old vicar had brought many years before from Italy and the vicar sat down in the vacant chair between them. Albert Edward faced them, the table between him and them and wondered with slight uneasiness what was the matter. He remembered still the occasion on which the organist had got in trouble and the bother they had all had to hush things up. In a church like St. Peter's, Neville Square, they couldn't afford scandal. On the vicar's red face was a look of resolute benignity but the others bore an expression that was slightly troubled.

"He's been naggin' them he 'as," said the verger to himself. "He's jockeyed them into doin' something, but they don't like it. That's what it is, you mark my words."

But his thoughts did not appear on Albert Edward's clean cut and distinguished features. He stood in a respectful but not **obsequious** attitude. He had been in service before he was appointed to his ecclesiastical office, but only in very good houses, and his deportment was irreproachable. Starting as a page-boy in the household of a merchant-prince he had risen by due degrees from the position of fourth to first footman, for a year he had been single-handed butler to a widowed peeress and, till the vacancy occurred at St. Peter's, butler with two men under him in the house of a retired ambassador. He was tall, spare, grave and dignified. He looked, if not like a duke, at least like an actor of the old school who specialised in dukes' parts. He had tact, firmness and self-assurance. His character was unimpeachable.

obsequious
too eager to praise or obey someone

The vicar began briskly.

"Foreman, we've got something rather unpleasant to say to you. You've been here a great many years and I think his lordship and the general agree with me that you've fulfilled the duties of your office to the satisfaction of everybody concerned."

The two churchwardens nodded.

"But a most extraordinary circumstance came to my knowledge the other day and I felt it my duty to impart it to the churchwardens. I discovered to my astonishment that you could neither read nor write."

The verger's face betrayed no sign of embarrassment.

"The last vicar knew that, sir," he replied. "He said it didn't make no difference. He always said there was a great deal too much education in the world for 'is taste."

"It's the most amazing thing I ever heard," cried the general. "Do you mean to say that you've been verger of this church for sixteen years and never learned to read or write?"

"I went into service when I was twelve sir. The cook in the first place tried to teach me once, but I didn't seem to 'ave the knack for it, and then what with one thing and another I never seemed to 'ave the time. I've never really found the want of it. I think a lot of these young fellows waste a rare lot of time readin' when they might be doin' something useful."

"But don't you want to know the news?" said the other churchwarden.

"Don't you ever want to write a letter?"

"No, me lord, I seem to manage very well without. And of late years now they've all these pictures in the papers I get to know what's goin' on pretty well. Me wife's quite a scholar and if I want to write a letter she writes it for me. It's not as if I was a bettin' man."

The two churchwardens gave the vicar a troubled glance and then looked down at the table.

"Well, Foreman, I've talked the matter over with these gentlemen and they quite agree with me that the situation is impossible. At a church like St. Peter's Neville Square, we cannot have a verger who can neither read nor write."

Albert Edward's thin, sallow face reddened and he moved uneasily on his feet, but he made no reply.

"Understand me, Foreman, I have no complaint to make against you. You do your work quite satisfactorily; I have the highest opinion both of your character and of your capacity; but we haven't the right to take the risk of some accident that might happen owing to your **lamentable** ignorance. It's a matter of **prudence** as well as of principle."

"But couldn't you learn, Foreman?" asked the general.

"No, sir, I'm afraid I couldn't, not now. You see, I'm not as young as I was and if I couldn't seem able to get the letters in me 'ead when I was a nipper I don't think there's much chance of it now."

"We don't want to be harsh with you, Foreman," said the vicar. "But the churchwardens and I have quite made up our minds. We'll give you three months and if at the end of that time you cannot read and write I'm afraid you'll have to go."

Albert Edward had never liked the new vicar. He'd said from the beginning that they'd made a mistake when they gave him St. Peter's. He wasn't the type

lamentable
regrettable; sorrowful

prudence
wisdom

of man they wanted with a classy congregation like that. And now he straightened himself a little. He knew his value and he wasn't going to allow himself to be put upon.

"I'm very sorry sir, I'm afraid it's no good. I'm too old a dog to learn new tricks. I've lived a good many years without knowin' 'ow to read and write, and without wishin' to praise myself, self-praise is no recommendation, I don't mind sayin' I've done my duty in that state of life in which it 'as pleased a merciful providence to place me, and if I could learn now I don't know as I'd want to."

"In that case, Foreman, I'm afraid you must go."

"Yes sir, I quite understand. I shall be 'appy to 'and in my resignation as soon as you've found somebody to take my place."

But when Albert Edward with his usual politeness had closed the church door behind the vicar and the two churchwardens he could not sustain the air of unruffled dignity with which he had borne the blow inflicted upon him and his lips quivered. He walked slowly back to the vestry and hung up on its proper peg his verger's gown. He sighed as he thought of all the grand funerals and smart weddings it had seen. He tidied everything up, put on his coat, and hat in hand walked down the aisle. He locked the church door behind him. He strolled across the square, but deep in his sad thoughts he did not take the street that led him home, where a nice strong cup of tea awaited; he took the wrong turning. He walked slowly along. His heart was heavy. He did not know what he should do with himself. He did not fancy the notion of going back to domestic service; after being his own master for so many years, for the vicar and churchwardens could say what they liked, it was he that had run St. Peter's, Neville Square, he could scarcely demean himself by accepting a situation. He had saved a tidy sum, but not enough to live on without doing something, and life seemed to cost more every year. He had never thought to be troubled with such questions. The vergers of St. Peter's, like the popes' Rome, were there for life. He had often thought of the pleasant reference the vicar would make in his sermon at evensong the first Sunday after his death to the long and faithful service, and the exemplary character of their late verger, Albert Edward Foreman. He sighed deeply. Albert Edward was a non-smoker and a total abstainer, but with a certain **latitude**; that is to say he liked a glass of beer with his dinner and when he was tired he enjoyed a cigarette. It occurred to him now that one would comfort him and since he did not carry them he looked about him for a shop where he could buy a packet of Gold Flakes. He did not at once see one and walked on a little. It was a long street with all sorts of shops in it, but there was not a single one where you could buy cigarettes. "That's strange," said Albert Edward.

latitude
freedom

To make sure he walked right up the street again. No, there was no doubt about it. He stopped and looked reflectively up and down.

"I can't be the only man as walks along this street and wants a fag," he said. "I shouldn't wonder but what a fellow might do very well with a little shop here. Tobacco and sweets, you know."

He gave a sudden start.

"That's an idea," he said. "Strange 'ow things come to you when you least expect it."

He turned, walked home, and had his tea.

"You're very silent this afternoon, Albert," his wife remarked.

"I'm thinkin'", he said.

He considered the matter from every point of view and next day he went along the street and by good luck found a little shop to let that looked as though it would exactly suit him. Twenty-four hours later he had taken it and when a month after that he left St. Peter's, Neville Square, forever, Albert Edward Foreman set up in business as a tobacconist and newsagent. His wife said it was a **dreadful** come-down after being verger of St. Peter's, but he answered that you had to move with the times, the church wasn't what it was, and 'enceforward he was going to render unto Caesar what was Caesar's. Albert Edward did very well. He did so well that in a year or so it struck him that he might take a second shop and put a manager in. He looked for another long street that hadn't got a tobacconist in it and when he found it and a shop to let, took it and stocked it. This was a success too. Then it occurred to him that if he could run two he could run half a dozen, so he began walking about London, and whenever he found a long street that had no tobacconist and a shop to let he took it. In the course of ten years he had acquired no less than ten shops and he was making money hand over fist. He went round to all of them himself every Monday, collected the week's takings and took them to the bank.

dreadful
frightful

One morning when he was there paying in a bundle of notes and a heavy bag of silver the cashier told him that the manager would like to see him. He was shown into an office and the manager shook hands with him.

"Mr. Foreman, I wanted to have a talk to you about the money you've got on deposit with us. D'you know exactly how much it is?"

"Not within a pound or two, sir; but I've got a pretty rough idea."

"Apart from what you paid in this morning it's a little over thirty thousand pounds. That's a very large sum to have on deposit and I should have thought you'd do better to invest it."

"I wouldn't want to take no risk, sir. I know it's safe in the bank."

"You needn't have the least anxiety. We'll make you out a list of absolutely gilt-edged securities. They'll bring you in a better rate of interest than we can possibly afford to give you." A troubled look settled on Mr. Foreman's distinguished face. "I've never 'ad anything to do with stocks and shares and I'd 'ave to leave it all in your 'ands," he said.

The manager smiled. "We'll do everything. All you'll have to do next time you come in is just to sign the transfers."

"I could do that all right," said Albert uncertainly. "But 'ow should I know what I was signin'?"

"I suppose you can read," said the manager a trifle sharply.

Mr. Foreman gave him a disarming smile.

"Well, sir, that's just it. I can't. I know it sounds funny-like but there it is, I can't read or write, only me name, an' I only learnt to do that when I went into business."

The manager was so surprised that he jumped up from his chair.

"That's the most extraordinary thing I ever heard."

"You see it's like this, sir, I never 'ad the opportunity until it was too late and then some'ow I wouldn't. I got obstinate-like."

prehistoric
belonging to a period before recorded history

aristocratic
upper-class

The manager stared at him as though he were a **prehistoric** monster.

"And do you mean to say that you've built up this important business and amassed a fortune of thirty thousand pounds without being able to read or write? Good God, man, what would you be now if you had been able to?"

"I can tell you that sir," said Mr. Foreman, a little smile on his still **aristocratic** features. "I'd be verger of St. Peter's, Neville Square."

Comprehension

1. What significance does Albert Edward Foreman attach to his verger's gown?
2. Why does the vicar feel that a verger like Foreman is not required at St. Peter's Neville Square?
3. How did Foreman become a successful businessman?
4. How does the bank manager react when he comes to know that Foreman managed to amass a fortune of thirty thousand pounds despite being illiterate?
5. What do you have to say about Albert Edward's final comment to the bank manager?

Structural Grammar

Adjectives

Use the words from the box and complete the sentences.

obsequious useful long rare disarming rough

1. Mr. Foreman gave him a ____________ smile.
2. He stood in a respectful but not ____________ attitude.
3. It was a ____________ street with all sorts of shops in it.
4. I think a lot of these young fellows waste a ____________ lot of time readin' when they might be doin' something ____________.
5. I've got a pretty ____________ idea.

The words you used in the above exercise are *adjectives*. Adjectives are words that describe nouns and pronouns. In '*red* ball', '*green* mountain' or '*beautiful* flower', *red*, *green*, and *beautiful* are adjectives.

Think and Write

Remember that success and failure are not measured by money alone. Maugham's story challenges the conventional notion of education. While the verger could neither read nor write, he could understand business opportunities, cash in on them, and expand and invest his wealth successfully. Yet, despite his talents, what he had wanted was to be a verger. It is interesting that the acquisition of wealth does not make the verger a greedy capitalist. Today, when economic hardships cause despair, and peer pressure and anxiety about material success drive so many to suicide, we forget that redefining our dreams is a great way of finding success.

Write the unusual success story of someone who has inspired you.

Listening

Tips for Goal-Setting

Listening Exercise 1

Listen to the talk about tips on goal-setting, then answer the following questions based on what you have just listened to. You may listen to the above talk again as you answer.

1. What is the prerequisite to achieving success?
2. What does WAST stand for?
3. What does PEER stand for?
4. How should a goal be stated?
5. What are the seven important areas for goal-setting?
6. What are the two types of goals?

Talking About Goals

Listening Exercise 2

Listen to the following speakers as they talk about their goals. Listen to the speakers again and answer the following:

- Write down three things that Geetha wishes to do.

____

____

____

- Write down three things that Aravind wishes to do.

____

____

____

- Write down three things that Priyanka wishes to do.

____

____

____

Speaking

Pair/Group Work: "What I Wish To Do"

Rank the following dreams in order of importance to you. After having discussed your priorities with your partner or in your group, add any other to this list.

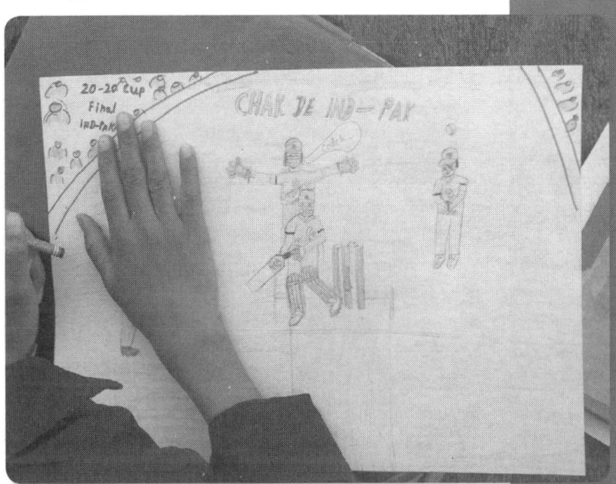

- Be happy
- Be honoured and respected
- Develop a particular talent or skill
- Enjoy loving relationships
- Enjoy comfort, leisure and recreation
- Have financial abundance
- Increase sense of purpose
- Live in a clean and beautiful environment
- Lead a healthy life
- ....
- ....
- ....
- 

Giving a Speech

Speaking Exercise 1

Choose one of the topics you strongly believe in from the list you and your partner made and give a speech. Make sure that you prepare notes on what should go into the introduction, body and conclusion of your speech.

In the introduction, make a clear statement.

In the body, explain the reasons for your opinion and give examples.

In the conclusion, reiterate your opinion and appeal for action.

Writing

Writing a Feature Story

A news story provides information about an event, idea or situation, whereas a feature article interprets news, adds depth and colour to a story, instructs or entertains.

Tips for Writing a Feature Story

Like an essay, a news story is divided into an introduction, body and conclusion.

1. In your introduction, you must entice your reader. Use drama, emotion, quotations, questions or descriptions.
2. In the body of the story, maintain the atmosphere that was created in the introduction.
3. In the conclusion, use a strong punch line to help the reader remember the story.

Some points to keep in mind:

1. Focus on human interest. Write the story in such a way that it arouses the feelings and emotions of your readers.
2. Be clear about why you are writing the story—is it to inform, persuade, observe, evaluate, or evoke emotion?
3. Write in the active voice to focus on what people *do*.
4. Keep your audience clearly in mind—what really matters to them?
5. Avoid clichés and sentimental statements.
6. Interviews for features usually need to be in-depth and in person rather than over the phone.
7. Use anecdotes and direct quotes to tell the story—try not to use too many paraphrases.
8. Talk to more than one person to provide a more complete picture.
9. Decide on the tense of your story at the start and stick to it. Present tense usually works best.
10. Avoid lengthy, complex paragraphs.

Writing Exercise 1

Interview some famous personalities and find out how they achieved success. Use the information about these famous people and add any other relevant details to write a special feature on tips for success for a newspaper or magazine.

Writing Exercise 2

Write an article titled "The World of My Dreams" for your college magazine.

Writing Exercise 3

Napoleon Hill said, "The starting point of all achievement is desire." Write to your friend explaining the importance of this statement.

Writing Exercise 4

Contrast lofty goals with ignoble ones. Give examples.

Vocabulary

Synonyms

Synonyms are different words with similar meanings. Words that are synonyms are said to be synonymous, and the state of being a synonym is called synonymy. An example of synonyms are the words 'brave' and 'courageous'.

Here are a few words and their synonyms:

Word	Synonyms
amazing	astonishing, surprising, stupefying, awesome, astounding, awe-inspiring
brilliant	superb, magnificent, glorious, bright, brainy
courageous	brave, daring, gutsy, plucky, valiant, audacious, spirited, bold
dazzling	glittering, stunning, impressive, astounding
fabulous	wonderful, tremendous, magnificent, marvellous, remarkable
gregarious	social, outgoing, extroverted, companionable, expressive
heinous	monstrous, shocking, dreadful, atrocious, awful, horrible
idiosyncratic	eccentric, peculiar, odd
lackadaisical	lazy, careless, laid-back

Find words that mean the same as the following:

1. contemptuous; scornful : ______________
2. imprisonment : ______________
3. handcuffs : ______________
4. banishment : ______________
5. search : ______________

6. penniless : ________________
7. leaps; jumps : ________________
8. deserted : ________________
9. boiling; scorching : ________________
10. dissatisfaction : ________________
11. revitalizing : ________________
12. doorstep : ________________
13. deteriorate : ________________
14. providence; fate : ________________
15. oath : ________________
16. violence; rough treatment : ________________
17. exhaustion; tiredness : ________________
18. misfortunes : ________________
19. harassment; maltreatment : ________________
20. hopelessness; anguish : ________________

Collocations

Collocations are combinations of words that are formed when two or more words are frequently used together in a way that sounds correct. For example, it is correct to say, "I'm under a bit of stress at the moment." However, it is wrong to say, "I'm below a bit of stress at the moment."

The words below collocate with a number of lexical items.

bright	sun; light; sky; idea; colour; red; future; prospects; child
goal	realistic; attainable; unrealistic; smart; silly; meaningful; specific; measurable; ignoble; worthy
harbour	doubt; grudges; uncertainty; suspicion
joyous	hymn; event; voice; daybreak; journey
lofty	ideas; ideals; sentiments; dreams; goals; thoughts
measurable	benefit; goal; progress
mighty	empire; kingdom; river; stream
radiant	sun; light; smile
realistic	plan; goal; idea; effect; model
take	a look; a holiday; a rest; a letter; time; notice; a walk

Complete the sentences below using the above words:

1. Vasantha is a woman of ____________ sentiments.
2. He felt great about participating in such a ____________ event.

3. Everyone thinks that he will have a ____________ future.
4. This product offers ____________ benefits to people's health.
5. Please ____________ time to study this section carefully.

Pronunciation

Word Stress

Listening Exercise 3

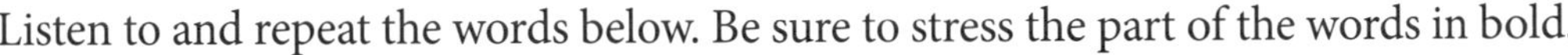

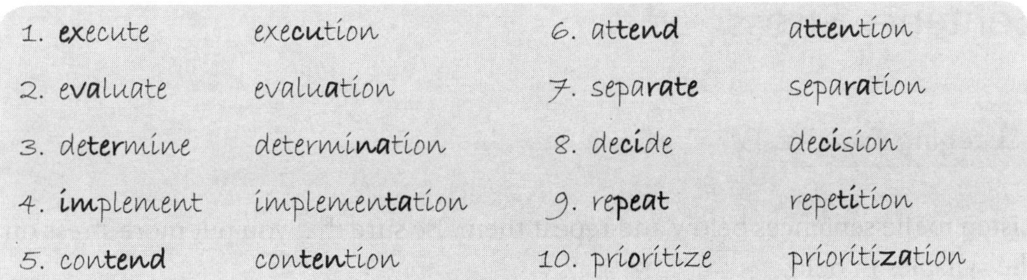

Pronunciation Tip

Most words that end in -ion are stressed on the second syllable from the end.

Syllables

A syllable is a single unit of speech, either a whole word, or one of the parts into which a word can be separated, and which usually contains a vowel sound. For instance, the word 'determination' has five syllables. They are *de, ter, mi, na,* and *tion.*

Words in English can be classified as **monosyllabic**, **disyllabic** or **polysyllabic**.

A **monosyllabic word** contains only one syllable; e.g., goal, set, short, long, aim, dream, etc.

A **disyllabic word** contains two syllables; e.g., decide, achieve, career, carrier, etc.

A **polysyllabic word** contains three or more syllables; e.g., ambition, determination, decision, implementation, etc.

Place the following words in the correct categories:

focus style balance control decide satisfaction
happy careful patience effort lofty ignoble

Monosyllabic	Disyllabic	Polysyllabic
____________	____________	____________
____________	____________	____________
____________	____________	____________
____________	____________	____________

Sentence Stress

Listening Exercise 4

Listen to the sentences below and repeat them. Be sure that you put more stress on the syllables in bold.

1. She **wants** to a**chieve** her **goals** **quick**ly.
2. Re**mem**ber to **write** your **goals** pre**cise**ly.
3. They pur**sued** their **dreams** with a **great** de**ter**mi**na**tion.
4. The **start**ing point of **all** a**chieve**ment is de**sire**.
5. He be**came** a **pro**minent perso**na**lity in a **sh**ort **ti**me.
6. We de**pen**ded on the **pro**ven **me**thods to at**tain** our **as**pi**ra**tions.
7. They prog**ress**ed re**mark**ably **well**.
8. We trans**form**ed our **li**ves **to**tally.
9. They **fa**ced **se**veral **trials** and tribu**la**tions.
10. He **show**ed an in**dom**itable **spi**rit and over**came** insur**moun**table **pro**blems.

Functional Grammar

Conditional Clauses

Conditional sentences are often used in spoken communication. You can use them to talk about a possible future occurrence, an unlikely situation or something that might have happened in the past, but did not actually happen. Study the following three types of conditional clauses:

First Conditional

Example:	"If you pursue your goals passionately, you will achieve success easily."
Form:	The *if-clause* is put in the present simple tense, and the main clause has a 'will'.
Use:	We use this type of sentence pattern when we express an intention. It is usually used in offers, suggestions, warnings and threats.
Examples:	"If we plan properly, we will accomplish our goals." "If we don't prioritize our goals, we won't achieve much."

Second Conditional

Example:	"If you pursued your goals passionately, you would achieve success easily."
Form:	The if-clause is in the simple past tense, and the main clause has a 'would'.
Use:	We use this type of sentence pattern when we express suppositions.

These suppositions can be:

Statements of unreal situations

"If I were you, I would be more goal-oriented." (I'm not you.)

Statements about we don't expect to happen

"If I had a magic wand, I would change the entire world." (But I don't really expect to have a magic wand.)

Third Conditional

Example:	"If you had pursued your goals passionately, you would have achieved success easily."
Form:	The if-clause is in the past perfect tense, and the main clause has a 'would have'.
Use:	We use this conditional to talk about things in the past happening differently from the way they really happened. This sometimes means criticizing people, pointing out their mistakes or expressing regret about the past.

Complete the following sentences by choosing the correct option:

First Conditional

1. If I become the prime minister of my country, I...

   a) would create more jobs.

   b) will create more jobs.

2. If you follow my advice, your...

   a) dreams will be fulfilled.

   b) dreams would be fulfilled.

3. If you set goals for different areas of life, you...

   a) would lead a balanced life.

   b) will lead a balanced life.

4. Our plans will come to fruition, if...

   a) we work meticulously.

   b) we will work meticulously.

5. If you don't have proper resources, you...

   a) will not fulfil your ambitions.

   b) wouldn't fulfil your ambitions.

Second Conditional

1. If Karan knew how to plan notes, he...

   a) will give a great speech.

   b) would give a great speech.

2. We would be much better off if we...

   a) had set right goals.

   b) would set right goals.

3. You would be glad, if you...

   a) would learn them on your own.

   b) learnt them on your own.

4. If I had a lot of money, I...

   a) bought myself a holiday resort.

   b) would buy myself a holiday resort.

5. Hemanth would be very upset, if...

   a) he knows about your plans.

   b) he knew about your plans.

Third Conditional

1. If I had learnt this technique earlier, I...

   a) would gain so much.

   b) would have gained so much.

2. We wouldn't have failed, if we...

   a) had executed our plans properly.

   b) will execute our plans properly.

3. Mohan's life wouldn't have gone out of control, if he...

   a) had balanced different areas of his life.

   b) balanced different areas of his life.

4. She wouldn't have messed up her life, if she...

   a) had gotten her priorities right.

   b) gotten her priorities right.

Mixed Conditionals

1. If people were more goal-oriented...
   a) our world would have been a better place.
   b) our world would be a better place.
   c) our world will be a better place.
2. If she had balanced her career and family, she...
   a) will be happier.
   b) would have been happier.
   c) would be happier.
3. If you lead a hectic life, your life...
   a) would be restless.
   b) will be restless.
   c) would have been restless.
4. I would never set out to do a task, if I...
   a) am not sure of its consequences.
   b) was not sure of its consequences.
   c) had not been sure of its consequences.
5. You will never be disappointed, if you...
   a) would learn to view things in proper perspective.
   b) learn to view things in proper perspective.
   c) had learnt to view things in proper perspective.

Pair Work/Group Work

Give at least three ideas of your own to complete the following statements:

1. If we were politicians,

   ____

   ____

   ____

2. If we were millionaires,

   ____

   ____

   ____

3. If we were aliens,

   ____

   ____

   ____

4. If we were birds,

   ____

   ____

   ____

5. If we were magicians,

   ____

   ____

   ____

Wish Clauses

You can use wish clauses when you would like things to be different from the way they actually are. Use the verb 'wish' to refer to how you would like things to be in the present, to talk about how you would like things to be in the future or to talk about the way things were in the past.

Wishes About the Present

If you want to talk about a situation in the present, you can use the following structure:

wish + past simple or continuous.

Examples:

1. I wish I had a bike.
2. I wish I remembered dates easily.

There is another structure that is used to talk about actions that take place in the present, but which you want to change in the future. This structure is used to talk about another person, and generally about things you don't like. The structure is as follows:

wish + would/could + V1.

For examples:

1. I wish you wouldn't be confused about your priorities.
2. I wish it would rain.

Wishes About the Future

When you talk about the future, you use the same structure as you use to talk about present states. The future you talk about cannot be changed, and so the situation is seen as unreal and has to be referred to using past tenses.

Examples:

1. I have to prepare the agenda for the meeting tomorrow. I wish I didn't have to prepare the agenda for the meeting tomorrow.
2. I'll have to do some extra work over the weekend. I wish I didn't have to do any extra work over the weekend.

Wishes About the Past

When you think about a situation in the past, naturally you can't do anything to change it. Therefore this is a way of expressing regret. The structure is wish + past perfect.

Examples:

1. I did not do the work as planned. I wish I had completed the work as planned.
2. Now we've failed get this done. I wish we had honoured the deadlines so that we could have been successful.

Complete the following sentences by choosing the correct option:

Wishes About the Present

1. We are living in a small flat. I wish we ________________ in an independent house.
2. I am too complacent. I wish I ________________.

Wishes About the Future

1. My uncle is coming to stay with me next week. I wish ________________.
2. I'm giving a speech in front of a large audience tomorrow. I wish ________________.

Wishes About the Past

1. I promised our friends we'd arrive on time. I wish ________________, because now they'll be waiting for us.
2. She failed to achieve her dreams because she was over-ambitious. I wish __________.

Spelling

Look at the sets of words below and circle the word with the correct spelling. Check your answers with the other members of your team. If you need to, use a good dictionary to find the correct spelling.

1.	prominent	praminant	promminent	promminant
2.	acheive	achieve	achiev	acheiv
3.	decision	desision	dicision	decition
4.	perceverance	perseverance	persavarance	perseverence
5.	profesional	proffessional	profesional	professional
6.	personality	parsanolity	persanality	personnality
7.	entrepreneur	entrpreneur	entreprenur	entreprener
8.	reiterrate	rieterate	reitterate	reiterate
9.	posible	possibel	possible	passible
10.	difference	differance	diference	defference

4

Dabbawallahs: Mumbai's Best Managed Business

In this unit

Reading
"Dabbawallahs: Mumbai's Best Managed Business" by Amberish K. Diwanji

Structural Grammar
Prepositions

Listening
A Conversation on Teamwork

Speaking
Working as a Team

Writing
Writing About Experiences

Vocabulary
Words That Describe Careers

Pronunciation
Minimal Pairs

Functional Grammar
Subject and Verb Agreement

Spelling

Have you heard of six-sigma quality efficiency or supply chain management? Modern firms hire highly paid professionals and purchase expensive software to achieve these goals. Some people manage to do these things without any such aid. Intelligent use of public transport, division of labour, and a cooperative management policy can achieve more than Wharton School graduates do. To know more, read the following report from rediff NEWS.

Reading

"Dabbawallahs: Mumbai's Best Managed Business" by Amberish K. Diwanji

Prince Charles is not the first person to show an interest in the dabbawallahs of Mumbai. In fact, the first time they actually shot to international fame was when his compatriots at the BBC did a documentary on them way back in the late seventies.

But it was in the 1990s, when the management **lexicon** became a part of daily life, that the interest in dabbawallahs, now synonymous with Mumbai's blurringly fast life, grew.

Today, they are **feted** regularly and invited to lecture students of business management. Corporate chiefs applaud them; management gurus use them as models.

lexicon
vocabulary; system of words common to a particular discipline

feted
celebrated

Raghunath Medge, President, Nutan Mumbai Tiffin Box Suppliers Charity Trust, who met Prince Charles on Tuesday, will be in Lucknow in January to address the students of the prestigious Indian Institute of Management. And, in between, some management students will be spending time with him.

So what makes the dabbawallahs so unique? And how do they work?

At the simplest, the dabbawallahs deliver home-cooked meals to individuals at their workplaces and return empty tiffin boxes to homes and, in some cases, caterers.

For this, they charge Rs 300 to Rs 350, that is, $ 6 to 7, a month.

The workforce of the Tiffin Box Suppliers Trust, the cooperative body that runs the system, is 5,000. Each tiffin box contains two or three containers, often carrying traditional Indian fare—rice, curry, chapattis, and vegetables. Housewives even send notes to their hubbies in these boxes.

The process begins early in the morning. Cooked food is picked up from houses and caterers by dabbawallahs and taken to the nearest railway station. There, the different tiffin boxes are sorted out for specific destination stations and loaded onto large, rectangular trays accordingly.

Each tray can hold up to 40 boxes. These trays then travel in local trains down to various stations. At each station, there are another set of dabbawallahs who quickly take the dabbas meant to be distributed in that area and push in dabbas meant for other stations.

A Mumbai local halts at a station for about 20 seconds or less and thus, the dabbawallahs have to work with precision and speed. During rush hour, it's a nightmare. Ask anyone who has done time on Mumbai locals.

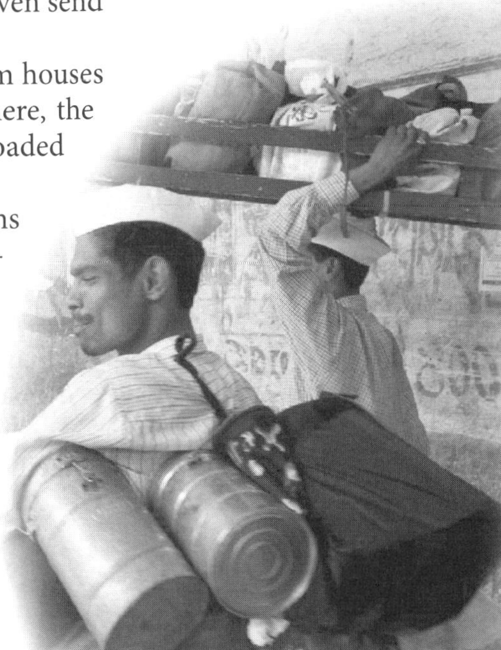

At each station, the boxes are once more sorted for localities and offices and taken there by handcarts or sometimes carried by individuals. "We carry up to 35 kg for distances of a couple of kilometres," points out Medge.

The boxes are placed in the offices' reception area by 12.30 pm and are picked up from the same spot by the deliverer a couple of hours later.

The whole process then starts again in the reverse. The boxes are picked up from the offices, taken to the nearest station and sorted for their journey home.

Forbes magazine gave this service its highest quality rating of Sigma 6, which means that per million transactions, there is just an error of one.

The service runs every working day.

"Every day, we deliver 175,000 to 200,000 lunch boxes," said Medge. "We use colours and code markings to ensure faultless delivery."

These codes would baffle a **cryptographer**! But they make perfect sense to the dabbawallahs. The codes and colours indicate the place from where a dabba is collected; the station where it must be unloaded and the office it is to be delivered.

cryptographer a person who cracks codes and cyphers

Explaining one part of the code, Medge said they use English letters to mark out stations—such as A for Andheri and Bo for Borivli.

The men who form part of the organisation are not employees. "If you have employees, then you have unions and strikes," said Medge, revealing his deep business acumen. "We are all shareholders in the Trust and we thus share in the earnings."

On an average, a dabbawallah can make about Rs 3,000 to 5,000. The Trust provides several services to its members, including schools for the children and health care in emergencies.

What makes the dabbawallahs an extremely tight-knit group is that they all hail from the same region, Pune district in Maharashtra. "We all come from the region east of the Sahyadri (Western Ghats), and everyone who joins us is known to us," said Medge.

"If an outsider does join in, we initially employ him on a fixed salary, and if in a couple of years he wins our trust, we may make him a shareholder," added Medge.

Only a handful of the Trust members are not from the Pune region and most of them are related to each other. They all share similar customs and traditions and worship Vithoba of Pandharpur.

"In fact, today is Prabhodini Ekadashi, when yatras (pilgrimages) to Pandharpur are made. So all our members will be fasting today," Medge explained.

Yet, while Vithoba is their presiding deity, their success is linked to the Mumbai suburban train network. On those odd days when the railways ground to a halt, the dabbas are not delivered.

But then, if Mumbai's locals aren't running, most Mumbaiites won't reach their offices.

Why have they not tried a similar service in other cities?

"Mumbai's geography makes it unique," Medge points out. "It is a longish city where residences are in the north and offices in the south, so it makes our work simple. We tried a similar service in Delhi a few years ago and it didn't work out; Delhi being a circular city, the logistics were difficult."

The dabbawallah service began way back in 1890, when Mumbai was a much smaller city. "At that time, migration of workers to the city had just begun and they wanted homemade food at their workplaces. Mumbai is a city with people from all over India, but the South Indians want their food, while the Gujaratis want their food. Our service began to fill this growing need," said Medge.

Today, the service delivers not just homemade food but also picks up food from caterers and delivers them to offices. But Medge said that food from caterers is still a small segment of the total operation. "Most people want to eat homemade food in the offices," he said.

As long as the dabbawallah service is there, Mumbaikars alone in the world would have the option of eating homemade food in office without the bother of having to carry a **cumbersome** lunchbox.

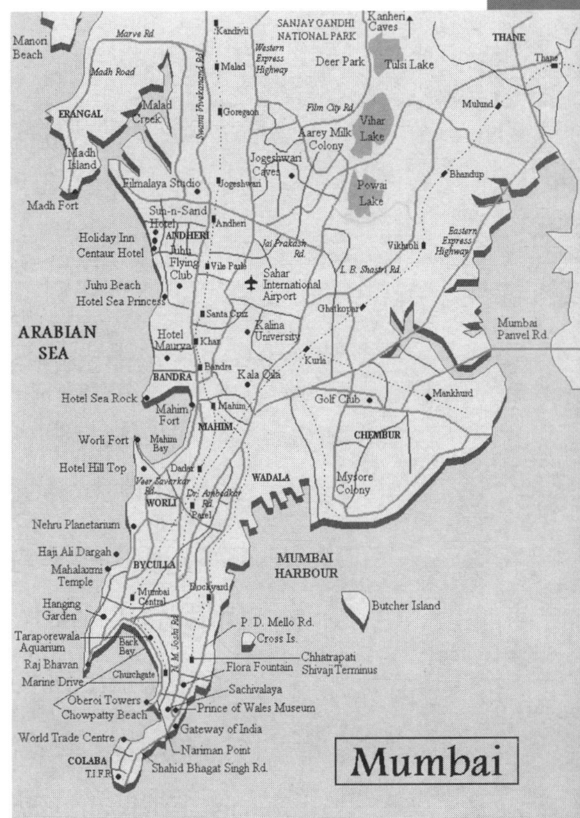

cumbersome
burdensome

Comprehension

1. When was the BBC documentary on Mumbai's dabbawallahs first shot?
2. What are the two external factors that help the dabbawallahs?
3. How does the team maintain its unity? Explain by citing two methods.
4. How does colour coding help the dabbawallahs?
5. What is a six-sigma rating?
6. How does the cosmopolitanism of Mumbai help the business of the dabbawallahs?

Structural Grammar

Prepositions

Fill in the blanks with appropriate prepositions:

for from in onto to

The process begins early ____________ the morning. Cooked food is picked up ____________ houses and caterers by dabbawallahs and taken ____________ the nearest railway station. There, the different tiffin boxes are sorted out ____________ specific destination stations and loaded ____________ large, rectangular trays accordingly.

Think and Write

The dabbawallahs of Mumbai use a teamwork model that functions well in a controlled environment. It is important to applaud the success of the dabbawallahs because theirs is a cooperative organization that is the highest form of a commercial team work enterprise. Teamwork also depends on social factors. In most corporate environments, multiculturalism is a big challenge. The dabbawallah model is hardly multicultural. To be truly successful, teamwork should not depend on supply chain logistics alone; the cultural limitations of the model should also be taken into account.

The above passage is an example of journal or news writing. Facts, views and analyses flow into the text. Even as the efforts of the dabbawallahs are praised, one is reminded that their success depends upon the suburban train service and the geography of Mumbai, and that they had failed to implement their model in Delhi.

Write a report on a great feat that was achieved through teamwork.

Listening

A Conversation on Teamwork

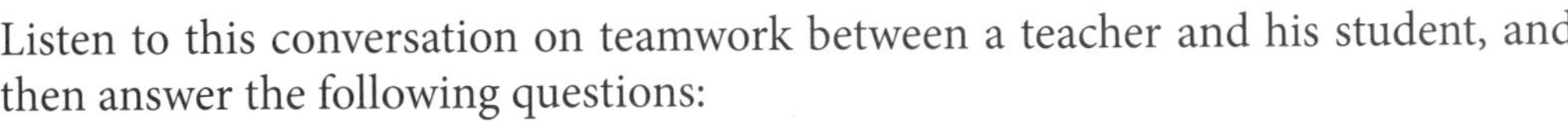

Listening Exercise 1

Listen to this conversation on teamwork between a teacher and his student, and then answer the following questions:

1. What is teamwork?

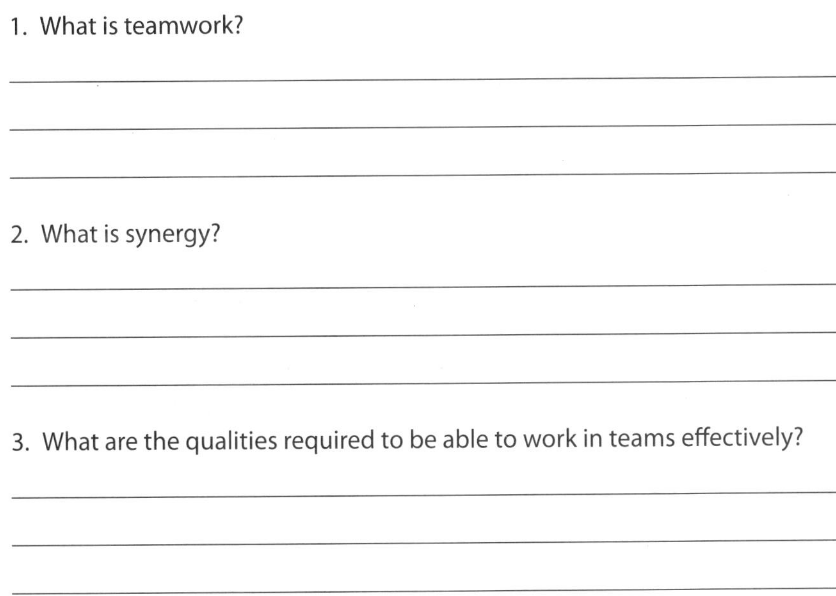

2. What is synergy?

3. What are the qualities required to be able to work in teams effectively?

Speaking

Working as a Team

Speaking Exercise 1

Things in Common

Form a small group of five or six members. Discuss and find out what you have in common as a team. Share them with other teams in the class. Use the space below to write about the things that the individuals in your group have in common.

Choosing a Team Leader

Play an interesting game of your choice and choose the winner as your team leader. Use the space below to describe the process involved.

___

___

___

Naming the Team

Now, the team leader is to ask each member to suggest an interesting name for the team, along with a good reason for their choice. After discussion and debate, each team should announce the name of their team and explain the reason for their choice.

Performing a Task

Have your team brainstorm on why employees of organizations want good team players. Also have a discussion in your team on what is that is required to be able to work in teams successfully. One member from the team will share their ideas with the class.

___

___

___

Talking About the Experience of Working in a Team

Now, describe in as much detail as possible your experience of working on the above tasks in your team. Share your experience with the class.

___

___

___

Writing

Writing About Experiences

Writing Exercise 1

Have you ever been a member of a committee, club or volunteer organization? Describe your experience of working in the team in as much detail as possible.

Vincent Lombardi says, "The achievements of an organization are the results of the combined effort of each individual." Write your opinion on this statement.

Vocabulary

Words That Describe Careers

Study the words and phrases related to careers given below:

calling	career training
career development	job
career diversity	new career
career ladder	profession
career management	vocation
career man/woman	work
career stages	

Work in teams and gather words related to the following:

Words denoting occupations and jobs

Words and phrases related to teamwork

____

____

____

Words and phrases related to the workplace

____

____

____

Pronunciation

Minimal Pairs

Minimal pairs are pairs of words or phrases whose pronunciation differs by one vowel or consonant sound, such as *seen* and *sin*, or *sheep* and *ship*.

Practise minimal pairs to enable you to speak English with clarity.

Listening Exercise 2

Listen to the words below and say them aloud:

1. **beam** ream seem team
2. **fame** game name shame
3. **cot** dot hot rot shot
4. **feel** heel meal seal zeal
5. **chick** lick pick sick tick
6. **beat** heat meet neat seat wheat
7. **bed** dead head led said wed

Make at least five minimal pairs each with the following the sets of words:

1. bite

2. lack

3. vote

4. perk

5. fan

Functional Grammar

Subject and Verb Agreement

1. When the subject of a sentence is singular, it takes a singular verb, and if the subject is plural, it takes a plural verb.

Example:

*Ganesh **goes** to work every day.*

*They **go** fishing every summer.*

2. When the subject of a sentence has two or more nouns or pronouns connected by 'and', a plural verb is used.

Example:

*Sushma, Monika and Sharat **enjoy** hiking.*

3. When a singular noun and a plural noun are joined by 'or' or 'nor', the noun that is closest to the verb determines whether the verb is singular or plural.

Example:

*Either Anand or his parents **are going** to come to the party.*

*Neither Anand's parents nor Anand **is going** to come to the party.*

4. The verb always agrees with the subject, even when a modifier gets in the way.

Example:

*The junior partner, who had invested much more than the others, **was** elated.*

5. The words 'each', 'each one', 'either', 'neither', 'everyone', 'everybody', 'anybody', 'anyone', 'nobody', 'somebody', 'someone', and 'no one' are singular and require a singular verb.

Example:

*Everybody **thinks** that Saritha is smart-looking.*

6. Some singular nouns have a plural form, such as trousers, scissors, glasses, pants, etc., and thus require a plural verb. When they are preceded by 'a pair of', however, they are treated as singular.

Example:

*Those trousers **are made** of cotton.*

*A pair of glasses **was** on the floor.*

7. In sentences beginning with 'there is' or 'there are', the subject follows the verb.

Example:

*There **are** many good leaders in our country.*

*There **is** one leader in our locality who is honest to the core.*

8. Collective nouns such as 'group', 'team', 'committee', 'class', and 'family' require a singular verb.

Example:

*The team **wants** to complete its project in time.*

*Ravi's family never **agrees** to what he needs to do.*

In some cases, however, a sentence may call for the use of a plural verb when using a collective noun.

Example:

*The team **have lost** the match.*

9. Some nouns have an '-s' ending but are singular, and require singular verbs.

Example:

*Physics **is** my favourite subject.*

*The doctor's diagnosis **was** not reassuring.*

Writing Exercise

Working in small groups, discuss what is wrong with the following sentences. Write the correct version in the space provided.

1. Shyam clock in at 9 o'clock every day.

2. Ramu and Ravi clocks out at 4 o'clock.

3. Swapna doesn't gets along with her colleagues.

4. Karan don't understand his position in the team clearly.

5. We doesn't like working in teams.

6. Brian have a bike.

7. There is twelve months in a year.

8. The news of the killing are spreading quickly.

9. The new student, along with the boss, were seen at the gate.

10. The reasons he give for his absence is silly.

11. All of them likes working in teams.

12. None of them are clear about how to go about the task.

13. Some of them wants to stay away from the meeting.

14. None of them want to go on a picnic.

15. Manoj's ability to lead the teams were appreciated by all.

____

16. These qualities helps you in achieving your goals.

____

17. Neither the team leader nor the members has understood the problem correctly.

____

18. The surface of some tables were damaged.

____

19. The equipment were broken.

____

20. The teams was reconstituted.

____

Spelling

Look at the sets of words below and circle the word with the correct spelling. Check your answers with the members of your team. If you need to, use a good dictionary to find the correct spelling.

1.	(compromise)	compromize	campromise	compramise
2.	consistancy	cansistency	consisstency	consislency
3.	defensive	deffensive	difensive	defenssive
4.	expartise	expertize	experteese	expertise
5.	oponent	opponant	opponent	oponant
6.	performence	performance	parformance	perrformance
7.	priparation	preparration	preparation	preparattion
8.	prevint	privent	prevvent	prevent
9.	relability	relaibility	relliability	reliability
10.	valunteer	volunter	vollunteer	volunteer

5

A Sea of Troubles

In this unit

Reading
"A Sea of Troubles" by P. G. Wodehouse
Structural Grammar
Articles
Listening
A Talk on Reducing Stress
Presentation Anxieties
Speaking
Stressful Events
Writing
Formal Letters
Vocabulary
Collocations of 'Stress' and 'Stressful'
Pronunciation
Word Stress
Sentence Stress
Functional Grammar
Active and Passive Voice
Direct and Indirect Speech
Expressing Suggestions
Spelling

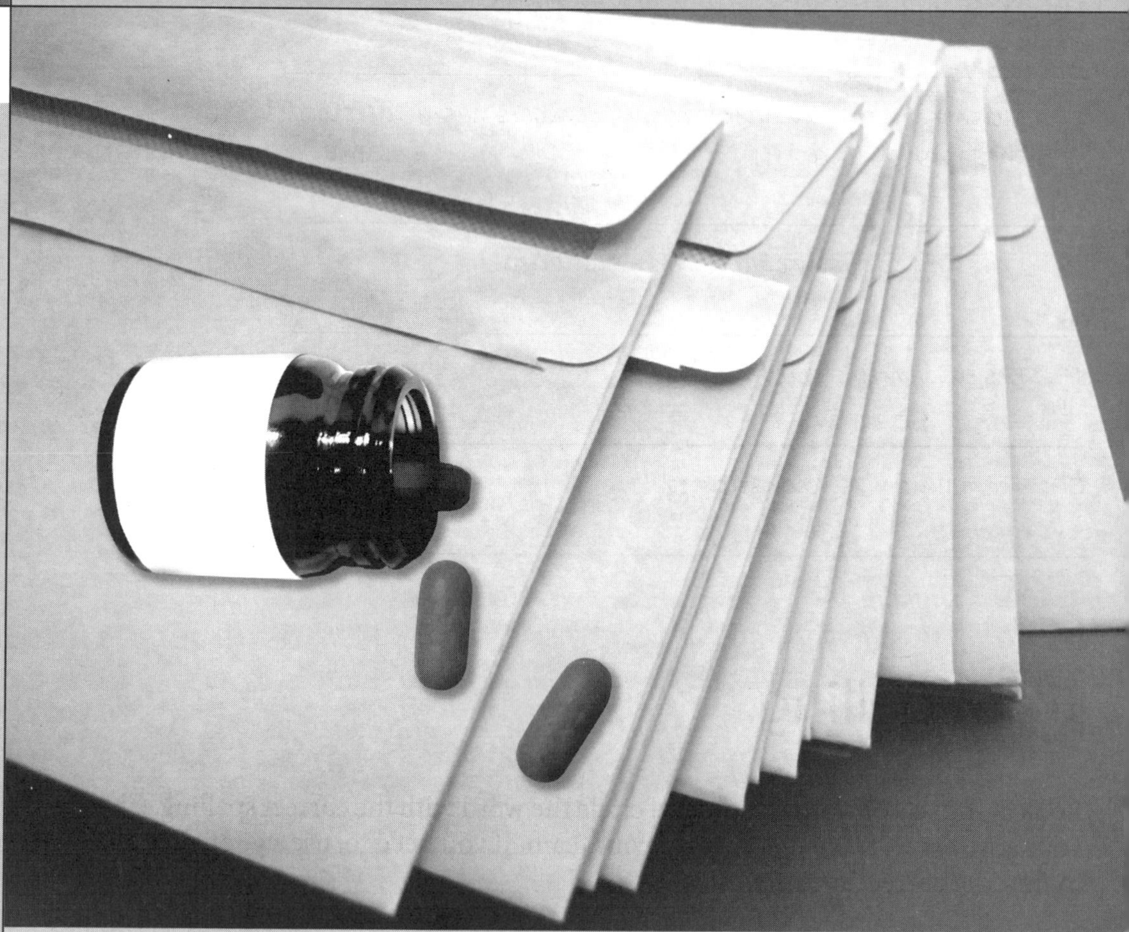

Suicide is perhaps the ghastliest way of ending life. Most would agree that there is nothing more precious than human life. We work, eat and sleep to ensure longer and happier lives. Yet in P. G. Wodehouse's *A Sea of Troubles* a man is driven to thoughts of suicide by indigestion! Written with Wodehouse's characteristic wit, this story is a hilarious read.

P. G. Wodehouse (1881–1975) is best known for his Jeeves and Blandings novels and stories. A master of English prose, he has been admired by generations of writers, including Rudyard Kipling and Salman Rushdie. In 1973, he was made a Knight of the British Empire.

Reading

"A Sea of Troubles" by P. G. Wodehouse

Mr Meggs's mind was made up. He was going to commit suicide.

There had been moments, in the interval which had elapsed between the first inception of the idea and his present state of fixed determination, when he had wavered. In these moments he had debated, with Hamlet, the question whether it was nobler in the mind to suffer, or to take arms against a sea of troubles and by opposing end them. But all that was over now. He was resolved.

Mr Meggs's point, the main plank, as it were, in his suicidal platform, was that with him it was beside the question whether or not it was nobler to suffer in the mind. The mind hardly entered into it at all. What he had to decide was whether it was worth while putting up any longer with the perfectly infernal pain in his stomach. For Mr Meggs was a martyr to indigestion. As he was also devoted to the pleasures of the table, life had become for him one long battle, in which, whatever happened, he always got the worst of it.

He was sick of it. He looked back down the vista of the years, and found therein no hope for the future. One after the other all the patent medicines in creation had failed him. Smith's Supreme Digestive Pellets—he had given them a more than fair trial. Blenkinsop's Liquid Life-Giver—he had drunk enough of it to float a ship. Perkins's Premier Pain-Preventer, strongly recommended by the sword-swallowing lady at Barnum and Bailey's—he had wallowed in it. And so on down the list. His interior organism had simply sneered at the lot of them.

"Death, where is thy sting?" thought Mr Meggs, and forthwith began to make his preparations.

Those who have studied the matter say that the tendency to commit suicide is greatest among those who have passed their fifty-fifth year, and that the rate is twice as great for unoccupied males as for occupied males. Unhappy Mr Meggs, accordingly, got it, so to speak, with both barrels. He was fifty-six, and he was perhaps the most unoccupied adult to be found in the length and breadth of the United Kingdom. He toiled not, neither did he spin. Twenty years before, an unexpected legacy had placed him in a position to indulge a natural taste for idleness to the utmost. He was, at that time, as regards his professional life, a clerk in a rather obscure shipping firm. Out of office hours he had a mild fondness for letters, which took the form of meaning to read right through the hundred best books one day, but actually contenting himself with the daily paper and an occasional magazine.

Such was Mr Meggs at thirty-six. The necessity for working for a living and a salary too small to permit of self-indulgence among the more

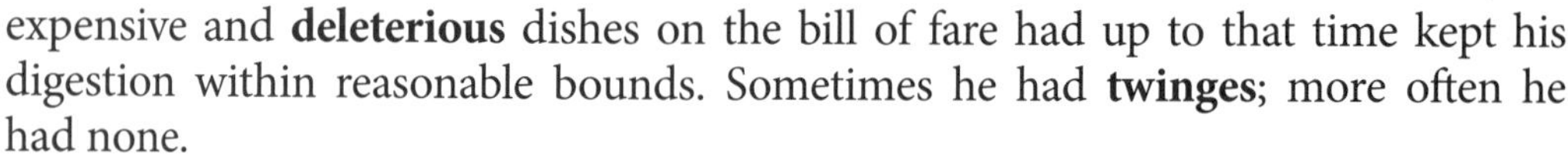

deleterious
harmful; damaging

twinge
a sharp sting of pain

sedentary
without exercise or activity; idle

dyspeptic
suffering from dyspepsia, that is, indigestion

expensive and **deleterious** dishes on the bill of fare had up to that time kept his digestion within reasonable bounds. Sometimes he had **twinges**; more often he had none.

Then came the legacy, and with it Mr Meggs let himself go. He left London and retired to his native village, where, with a French cook and a series of secretaries to whom he dictated at long intervals occasional paragraphs of a book on British Butterflies on which he imagined himself to be at work, he passed the next twenty years. He could afford to do himself well, and he did himself extremely well. Nobody urged him to take exercise, so he took no exercise. Nobody warned him of the perils of lobster and Welsh rabbits to a man of **sedentary** habits, for it was nobody's business to warn him. On the contrary, people rather encouraged the lobster side of his character, for he was a hospitable soul and liked to have his friends dine with him. The result was that Nature, as is her wont, laid for him, and got him. It seemed to Mr Meggs that he woke one morning to find himself a chronic **dyspeptic**. That was one of the hardships of his position, to his mind. The thing seemed to hit him suddenly out of a blue sky. One moment, all appeared to be peace and joy; the next, a lively and irritable wild-cat with red-hot claws seemed somehow to have introduced itself into his interior.

So Mr Meggs decided to end it.

In this crisis of his life the old methodical habits of his youth returned to him. A man cannot be a clerk in even an obscure firm of shippers for a great length of time without acquiring system, and Mr Meggs made his preparations calmly and with a forethought worthy of a better cause.

And so we find him, one glorious June morning, seated at his desk, ready for the end.

Outside, the sun beat down upon the orderly streets of the village. Dogs dozed in the warm dust. Men who had to work went about their toil moistly, their minds far away in shady public-houses.

But Mr Meggs, in his study, was cool both in mind and body.

Before him, on the desk, lay six little slips of paper. They were bank-notes, and they represented, with the exception of a few pounds, his entire worldly wealth. Beside them were six letters, six envelopes, and six postage stamps. Mr Meggs surveyed them calmly.

He would not have admitted it, but he had had a lot of fun writing those letters. The deliberation as to who should be his heirs had occupied him pleasantly for several days, and, indeed, had taken his mind off his internal pains at times so thoroughly that he had frequently surprised himself in an almost cheerful mood. Yes, he would have denied it, but it had been great sport sitting in his arm-chair, thinking whom he should pick out from England's teeming millions to make happy with his money. All sorts of schemes had passed through his mind. He had a sense of power which the mere possession of the money had never given him. He began to understand why millionaires make freak wills. At one time he had toyed with the idea of selecting someone at random from the London Directory and bestowing on him all he had to bequeath. He had only abandoned the scheme when it occurred to him that he himself would not be

in a position to witness the recipient's stunned delight. And what was the good of starting a thing like that, if you were not to be in at the finish?

Sentiment succeeded whimsicality. His old friends of the office—those were the men to benefit. What good fellows they had been! Some were dead, but he still kept intermittently in touch with half a dozen of them. And—an important point—he knew their present addresses.

This point was important, because Mr Meggs had decided not to leave a will, but to send the money direct to the beneficiaries. He knew what wills were. Even in quite straightforward circumstances they often made trouble. There had been some slight complication about his own legacy twenty years ago. Somebody had contested the will, and before the thing was satisfactorily settled the lawyers had got away with about twenty per cent of the whole. No, no wills. If he made one, and then killed himself, it might be upset on a plea of insanity. He knew of no relative who might consider himself entitled to the money, but there was the chance that some remote cousin existed; and then the comrades of his youth might fail to collect after all.

He declined to run the risk. Quietly and by degrees he had sold out the stocks and shares in which his fortune was invested, and deposited the money in his London bank. Six piles of large notes, dividing the total into six equal parts; six letters couched in a strain of reminiscent pathos and manly resignation; six envelopes, legibly addressed; six postage-stamps; and that part of his preparations was complete. He licked the stamps and placed them on the envelopes; took the notes and inserted them in the letters; folded the letters and thrust them into the envelopes; sealed the envelopes; and unlocking the drawer of his desk produced a small, black, ugly-looking bottle.

He opened the bottle and poured the contents into a medicine-glass.

It had not been without considerable thought that Mr Meggs had decided upon the method of his suicide. The knife, the pistol, the rope—they had all presented their charms to him. He had further examined the merits of drowning and of leaping to destruction from a height.

There were flaws in each. Either they were painful, or else they were messy. Mr Meggs had a tidy soul, and he revolted from the thought of spoiling his figure, as he would most certainly do if he drowned himself; or the carpet, as he would if he used the pistol; or the pavement—and possibly some innocent pedestrian, as must infallibly occur should he leap off the Monument. The knife was out of the question. Instinct told him that it would hurt like the very dickens.

No; poison was the thing. Easy to take, quick to work, and on the whole rather agreeable than otherwise.

Mr Meggs hid the glass behind the inkpot and rang the bell.

"Has Miss Pillenger arrived?" he inquired of the servant.

"She has just come, sir."

"Tell her that I am waiting for her here."

Jane Pillenger was an institution. Her official position was that of private secretary and typist to Mr Meggs. That is to say, on the rare occasions when Mr Meggs's conscience overcame his indolence to the extent of forcing him to resume work on his British Butterflies, it was to Miss Pillenger that he addressed the few rambling and incoherent remarks which constituted his idea of a regular hard, slogging spell of literary composition. When he sank back in his chair, speechless and exhausted like a Marathon runner who has started his sprint a mile or two too soon, it was Miss Pillenger's task to unscramble her shorthand notes, type them neatly, and place them in their special drawer in the desk.

austere
without indulgence or luxuries; uninvolved and self restrained

Miss Pillenger was a wary spinster of **austere** views, uncertain age, and a deep-rooted suspicion of men—a suspicion which, to do an abused sex justice, they had done nothing to foster. Men had always been almost coldly correct in their dealings with Miss Pillenger. In her twenty years of experience as a typist and secretary she had never had to refuse with scorn and indignation so much as a box of chocolates from any of her employers. Nevertheless, she continued to be icily on her guard. The clenched fist of her dignity was always drawn back, ready to swing on the first male who dared to step beyond the bounds of professional civility.

Such was Miss Pillenger. She was the last of a long line of unprotected English girlhood which had been compelled by straitened circumstances to listen for hire to the appallingly dreary nonsense which Mr Meggs had to impart on the subject of British Butterflies. Girls had come, and girls had gone, blondes, ex-blondes, brunettes, ex-brunettes, near-blondes, near-brunettes; they had come buoyant, full of hope and life, tempted by the lavish salary which Mr Meggs had found himself after a while compelled to pay; and they had dropped off, one after another, like exhausted bivalves, unable to endure the crushing boredom of life in the village which had given Mr Meggs to the world. For Mr Meggs's home-town was no City of Pleasure. Remove the Vicar's magic-lantern and the try-your-weight machine opposite the post office, and you practically eliminated the temptations to tread the primrose path. The only young men in the place were silent, gaping youths, at whom lunacy commissioners looked sharply and suspiciously when they met. The tango was unknown, and the one-step. The only form of dance extant—and that only at the rarest intervals—was a sort of polka not unlike the movements of a slightly inebriated boxing kangaroo. Mr Meggs's secretaries and typists gave the town one startled, horrified glance, and stampeded for London like frightened ponies.

Not so Miss Pillenger. She remained. She was a business woman, and it was enough for her that she received a good salary. For five pounds a week she would have undertaken a post as secretary and typist to a Polar Expedition. For six years she had been with Mr Meggs, and doubtless she looked forward to being with him at least six years more.

Perhaps it was the pathos of this thought which touched Mr Meggs, as she sailed, notebook in hand, through the doorway of the study. Here, he told himself, was a confiding girl, all unconscious of impending doom, relying on him as a daughter relies on her father. He was glad that he had not forgotten Miss Pillenger when he was making his preparations.

He had certainly not forgotten Miss Pillenger. On his desk beside the letters lay a little pile of notes, amounting in all to five hundred pounds—her legacy.

Miss Pillenger was always business-like. She sat down in her chair, opened her notebook, moistened her pencil, and waited expectantly for Mr Meggs to dear his throat and begin work on the butterflies. She was surprised when, instead of frowning, as was his invariable practice when bracing himself for composition, he bestowed upon her a sweet, slow smile.

All that was maidenly and defensive in Miss Pillenger leaped to arms under that smile. It ran in and out among her nerve-centres. It had been long in arriving, this moment of crisis, but here it undoubtedly was at last. After twenty years an employer was going to court disaster by trying to flirt with her.

Mr Meggs went on smiling. You cannot classify smiles. Nothing lends itself so much to a variety of interpretations as a smile. Mr Meggs thought he was smiling the sad, tender smile of a man who, knowing himself to be on the brink of the tomb, bids farewell to a faithful employee. Miss Pillenger's view was that he was smiling like an abandoned old rip who ought to have been ashamed of himself.

"No, Miss Pillenger," said Mr Meggs, "I shall not work this morning. I shall want you, if you will be so good, to post these six letters for me."

Miss Pillenger took the letters. Mr Meggs surveyed her tenderly.

"Miss Pillenger, you have been with me a long time now. Six years, is it not? Six years. Well, well. I don't think I have ever made you a little present, have I?"

"You give me a good salary."

"Yes, but I want to give you something more. Six years is a long time. I have come to regard you with a different feeling from that which the ordinary employer feels for his secretary. You and I have worked together for six long years. Surely I may be permitted to give you some token of my appreciation of your fidelity." He took the pile of notes. "These are for you, Miss Pillenger."

He rose and handed them to her. He eyed her for a moment with all the sentimentality of a man whose digestion has been out of order for over two decades. The pathos of the situation swept him away. He bent over Miss Pillenger, and kissed her on the forehead.

Smiles excepted, there is nothing so hard to classify as a kiss. Mr Meggs's notion was that he kissed Miss Pillenger much as some great general, wounded unto death, might have kissed his mother, his sister, or some particularly sympathetic aunt; Miss Pillenger's view, differing substantially from this, may be outlined in her own words.

"Ah!" she cried, as, dealing Mr Meggs's conveniently placed jaw a blow which, had it landed an inch lower down, might have knocked him out, she sprang to her feet. "How dare you! I've been waiting for this Mr Meggs. I have seen it in your eye. I have expected it. Let me tell you that I am not at all the sort of girl with whom it is safe to behave like that. I can protect myself. I am only a working-girl—"

Mr Meggs, who had fallen back against the desk as a stricken pugilist falls on the ropes, pulled himself together to protest.

"Miss Pillenger," he cried, aghast, "You misunderstand me. I had no intention—"

"Misunderstand you? Bah! I am only a working-girl—"

"Nothing was farther from my mind—"

"Indeed! Nothing was farther from your mind! You give me money, you shower your vile kisses on me, but nothing was farther from your mind than the obvious interpretation of such behaviour!" Before coming to Mr Meggs, Miss Pillenger had been secretary to an Indiana novelist. She had learned style from the master. "Now that you have gone too far, you are frightened at what you have done. You well may be, Mr Meggs. I am only a working-girl—"

"Miss Pillenger, I implore you—"

"Silence! I am only a working-girl—"

A wave of mad fury swept over Mr Meggs. The shock of the blow and still more of the frightful ingratitude of this horrible woman nearly made him foam at the mouth.

"Don't keep on saying you're only a working-girl," he bellowed. "You'll drive me mad. Go. Go away from me. Get out. Go anywhere, but leave me alone!"

Miss Pillenger was not entirely sorry to obey the request. Mr Meggs's sudden fury had startled and frightened her. So long as she could end the scene victorious, she was anxious to withdraw.

"Yes, I will go," she said, with dignity, as she opened the door. "Now that you have revealed yourself in your true colours, Mr Meggs, this house is no fit place for a wor—"

She caught her employer's eye, and vanished hastily.

Mr Meggs paced the room in a ferment. He had been shaken to his core by the scene. He boiled with indignation. That his kind thoughts should have been so misinterpreted—it was too much. Of all ungrateful worlds, this world was the most—

He stopped suddenly in his stride, partly because his shin had struck a chair, partly because an idea had struck his mind.

Hopping madly, he added one more parallel between himself and Hamlet by soliloquizing aloud.

"I'll be hanged if I commit suicide," he yelled.

And as he spoke the words a curious peace fell on him, as on a man who has awakened from a nightmare. He sat down at the desk. What an idiot he had been ever to contemplate self-destruction. What could have induced him to do it? By his own hand to remove himself, merely in order that a pack of ungrateful brutes might wallow in his money—it was the scheme of a perfect fool.

He wouldn't commit suicide. Not if he knew it. He would stick on and laugh at them. And if he did have an occasional pain inside, what of that? Napoleon had them, and look at him. He would be blowed if he committed suicide.

With the fire of a new resolve lighting up his eyes, he turned to seize the six letters and rifle them of their contents.

They were gone.

It took Mr Meggs perhaps thirty seconds to recollect where they had gone to, and then it all came back to him. He had given them to the demon Pillenger, and, if he did not overtake her and get them back, she would mail them.

Of all the mixed thoughts which seethed in Mr Meggs's mind at that moment, easily the most prominent was the reflection that from his front door to the post office was a walk of less than five minutes.

***

Miss Pillenger walked down the sleepy street in the June sunshine, boiling, as Mr Meggs had done, with indignation. She, too, had been shaken to the core. It was her intention to fulfil her duty by posting the letters which had been entrusted to her, and then to quit for ever the service of one who, for six years a model employer, had at last forgotten himself and showed his true nature.

Her meditations were interrupted by a hoarse shout in her rear; and, turning, she perceived the model employer running rapidly towards her. His face was scarlet, his eyes wild, and he wore no hat.

Miss Pillenger's mind worked swiftly. She took in the situation in a flash. Unrequited, guilty love had sapped Mr Meggs's reason, and she was to be the victim of his fury. She had read of scores of similar cases in the newspapers. How little she had ever imagined that she would be the heroine of one of these dramas of passion.

She looked for one brief instant up and down the street. Nobody was in sight. With a loud cry she began to run.

"Stop!"

It was the fierce voice of her pursuer. Miss Pillenger increased to third speed. As she did so, she had a vision of headlines.

"Stop!" roared Mr Meggs.

"UNREQUITED PASSION MADE THIS MAN MURDERER," thought Miss Pillenger.

"Stop!"

"CRAZED WITH LOVE HE SLAYS BEAUTIFUL BLONDE," flashed out in letters of crimson on the back of Miss Pillenger's mind.

"Stop!"

"SPURNED, HE STABS HER THRICE."

To touch the ground at intervals of twenty yards or so—that was the ideal she strove after. She addressed herself to it with all the strength of her powerful mind.

In London, New York, Paris, and other cities where life is brisk, the spectacle of a hatless gentleman with a purple face pursuing his secretary through the streets at a rapid gallop would, of course, have excited little, if any, remark. But in Mr Meggs's home-town events were of rarer occurrence. The last milestone in the history of his native place had been the visit, two years before, of Bingley's Stupendous Circus, which had paraded along the main street on its way to the next town, while zealous members of its staff visited the back premises of the houses and removed all the washing from the lines. Since then deep peace had reigned.

Gradually, therefore, as the chase warmed up, citizens of all shapes and sizes began to assemble. Miss Pillenger's screams and the general appearance of Mr Meggs gave food for thought. Having brooded over the situation, they decided at length to take a hand, with the result that as Mr Meggs's grasp fell upon Miss Pillenger the grasp of several of his fellow-townsmen fell upon him.

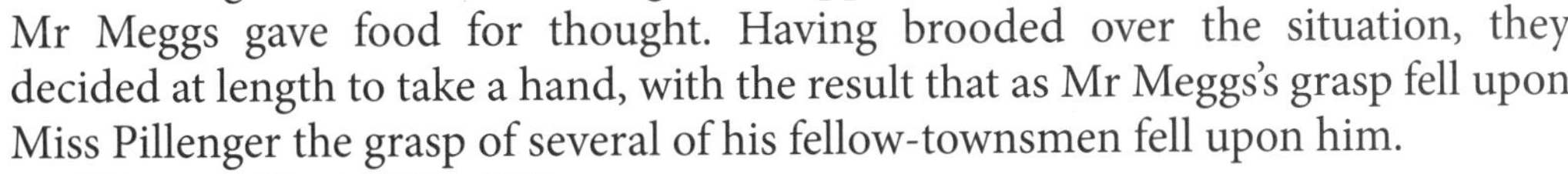

"Save me!" said Miss Pillenger.

Mr Meggs pointed speechlessly to the letters, which she still grasped in her right hand. He had taken practically no exercise for twenty years, and the pace had told upon him.

Constable Gooch, guardian of the town's welfare, tightened his hold on Mr Meggs's arm, and desired explanations.

"He—he was going to murder me," said Miss Pillenger.

"Kill him," advised an austere bystander.

"What do you mean you were going to murder the lady?" inquired Constable Gooch.

Mr Meggs found speech.

"I—I—I—I only wanted those letters."

"What for?"

"They're mine."

"You charge her with stealing 'em?"

"He gave them me to post with his own hands," cried Miss Pillenger.

"I know I did, but I want them back."

By this time the constable, though age had to some extent dimmed his sight, had recognized beneath the perspiration, features which, though they were distorted, were nevertheless those of one whom he respected as a leading citizen.

Why, Mr Meggs!" he said.

This identification by one in authority calmed, if it a little disappointed, the crowd. What it was they did not know, but, it was apparently not a murder, and they began to drift off.

"Why don't you give Mr Meggs his letters when he asks you, ma'am?" said the constable.

Miss Pillenger drew herself up **haughtily**.

haughtily
with an expression of pride and self-importance

"Here are your letters, Mr Meggs, I hope we shall never meet again."

Mr Meggs nodded. That was his view, too.

All things work together for good. The following morning Mr Meggs awoke from a dreamless sleep with a feeling that some curious change had taken place in him. He was abominably stiff, and to move his limbs was pain, but down in the centre of his being there was a novel sensation of lightness. He could have declared that he was happy.

Wincing, he dragged himself out of bed and limped to the window. He threw it open. It was a perfect morning. A cool breeze smote his face, bringing with it pleasant scents and the soothing sound of God's creatures beginning a new day.

An astounding thought struck him.

"Why, I feel well!"

Then another.

"It must be the exercise I took yesterday. By George, I'll do it regularly."

He drank in the air luxuriously. Inside him, the wild-cat gave him a sudden claw, but it was a half-hearted effort, the effort of one who knows that he is beaten. Mr Meggs was so absorbed in his thoughts that he did not even notice it.

"London," he was saying to himself. "One of these physical culture places... Comparatively young man... Put myself in their hands... Mild, regular exercise..."

He limped to the bathroom.

Comprehension

1. What was Mr Meggs's occupation before retiring to the village?
2. Why did Mr Meggs decide not to draft a will?
3. Describe the character of Miss Pillenger. Why did she tolerate the village life and its lack of action?
4. How would you describe Miss Pillenger's attitude?
5. Describe the character of the villagers.
6. Why does Mr Meggs decide not to commit suicide?

Think and Write

The above story is humorous. It also says a few things about stress, urban upper-class life, and restraining one's instincts. Both Meggs and Pillenger take things to extremes. Meggs wants to commit suicide to cure his indigestion, and Pillenger mistakes a kind employer of six years for a murderer. Humour writing often uses stereotypes and characters whose actions are exaggerated, and the language oscillates between overstatement and understatement.

With this in mind, write a humorous story of your own.

Structural Grammar

Articles

Correct the following sentences:

1. Out of office he had mild fondness for letters.
2. A cool breeze smote his face, bringing with it pleasant scents and soothing sound of God's creatures beginning a new day.
3. Miss Pillenger increased to the third speed. As she did so, she had vision of headlines.
4. He stopped suddenly in his stride, partly because his shin had struck chair, partly because a idea had struck his mind.
5. He had run very hard. He had taken practically no exercise for twenty years, and pace had told upon him.

Listening

A Talk on Reducing Stress

Listening Exercise 1

Listen to this talk in which a speaker gives some tips on reducing stress. Answer these questions based on the talk you have listened to.

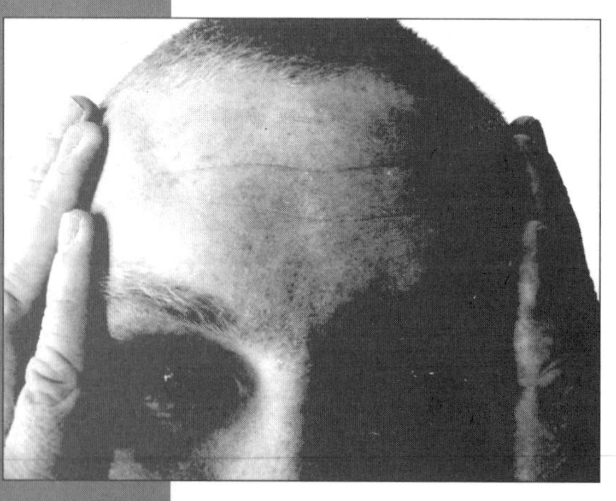

- What are the positive effects of stress?

  ____

  ____

  ____

- What are the negative effects of stress?

  ____

  ____

  ____

- What does managing stress involve?

  ____

  ____

  ____

- What are the four areas that need attention for effectively dealing with stress?

- List five points from the talk that appeal to you the most.

Presentation Anxieties

Listening Exercise 2

Listen to the conversation between a teacher and his student on presentation anxieties, then answer the following questions:

- What is the structure of a presentation?

- What are the tools and methods used to make presentations?

- What should be done to overcome stage fright?

- What should be done to ensure effective delivery of a presentation?

- Which aspects of language are important for presentations?

- How does one effectively handle the question and answer session?

____

____

____

- What are the criteria for assessing a presentation?

____

____

____

Speaking

Pair/Group Work: Stressful Events

Rank the following stressful events in order of seriousness after discussing them with your partner or your group. Add any other events you can think of that also cause stress.

- Death in the family
- Family problems
- Job loss
- Major injury or illness
- Unsatisfactory job

Speaking Exercise 1

Imagine that you are lost in a large city. You are looking for a particular hotel called Minerva Grand. Use words like 'who', 'how', 'where', 'please', and 'what' to ask for directions. We have given you the responses that you might receive from bystanders or passers-by. Based on them, form your questions and responses, and say them aloud.

Bystander 1: It is in Secunderabad. You can take a bus.

Bystander 2: It is forty kilometres from the airport.

Bystander 3: Which Minerva are you talking about? There is one in Himayatnagar too.

Bystander 4: From Abids, an autorickshaw will charge you around fifty rupees.

Speaking Exercise 2

Share what you feel about giving speeches and presentations with the class. You can use the space below to jot down your notes for your talk.

____

____

____

Writing

Formal Letters

The letters you write to friends and family are called informal letters, while the letters you write to business people and officials are considered formal letters. Most business letters have the following parts:

1. Heading

   This will include the name and contact details such as telephone and fax numbers, and the e-mail or Web address of the sender of the letter.

2. Date

   Since different parts of the world follow different date formats, it is best that you follow an alphanumeric format like '15 September 1992' for your letters.

3. Reference Number

   This again is an alphanumeric notation and helps in the filing of the letter, and is also useful for reference in future correspondence. This is a descriptive label and will be named as such in the letter.

4. Inside Address

   This will include the name (optionally) and the address of the proposed addressee of the letter. Remember to include the designation along with the name if your letter is meant for an individual.

5. Salutation

   You may use "Dear", followed the designation and name of the addressee. Remember to use the surname since this is a formal communication. Often, people use the entire name in their salutation. This applies if you choose not to sound too informal. So, instead of writing "Dear George" you could write "Dear Mr George Varghese". If you do not know the name of the addressee, you can choose to write "Dear Sir or Madam".

6. Subject Line

   This should be a short phrase clarifying the purpose of your letter. This is a descriptive label in the letter.

7. Body

    The main text of your letter should be precise, concise, and to the point.

8. Complimentary Close

    You can use 'Truly' or 'Sincerely', but use 'Yours' only if you also used 'Dear' in the salutation.

9. Signature Area

    Remember to sign your letter, and write your name below your signature. You should also mention your designation.

10. Enclosure Notation

    This includes common notations to indicate carbon copies, enclosed documents, etc.

Types of Formats

Full Block Format

In this business letter format, the entire letter is left aligned and single spaced except for a double space between paragraphs.

Modified Block Letter Format

In the modified block style the return address, date, complimentary closing and the signature line are slightly to the right of the centre of the letter.

Semi-block Letter Format

In the semi-block style indents the return address, date and complimentary closing are aligned slightly to the right of the centre of the letter. Additionally, the subject line and each paragraph in the body of the letter are also indented. This is done to draw the reader's attention to the main issues raised in the letter.

Abbreviations Used in Letter Writing

The following abbreviations are widely used in letters:

cc	carbon copy (when you send a copy of a letter to more than one person, you use this abbreviation to let them know)
enc.	enclosure (when you include other papers with your letter)
pp	per procurationem (a Latin phrase meaning that you are signing the letter on somebody else's behalf)
ps	postscript (when you want to add something after you've finished and signed the letter)
RSVP	please reply

Full Block Format

Sample of full block letter with elements

[Your street address] 1
[City, state and PIN code]
[Phone number (including STD code)]
[Email address]

[Today's date] 2

Reference Number: [Add reference number] 3

[Name of addressee] 4
[Title or position]
[Street address]
[City, state and PIN code]

Dear [Addressee's name]: 5

[SUBJECT] 6

[Body of letter in paragraph form 7
In the block format, the first lines of paragraphs are not indented, although a blank space separates each paragraph.]

[If your letter continues to more than one page, type the complimentary close on the last page of the letter.]

Yours sincerely (or truly), 8

[Your signature] 9
[Your name, designation]

Enclosure(s): i. [Mention details] 10
ii. [Mention details]

Writing Exercise 1

1. Write a letter to the principal of your college for permission to go on a 10-day excursion to Kerala.
2. Write a letter to the Chief Electrical Engineer, APTRANSCO, to complain about the low voltage in your area.
3. Write a letter of complaint to the manager of Hind Electronics on the faulty functioning of a recently purchased refrigerator.

Vocabulary

Collocations of 'Stress' and 'Stressful'

Study the following collocations with 'stress' and 'stressful' and use them in your speech and writing.

stress level / reduction / buster / sign / symptom / indicator / warning

cause / reduce / combat / fight / manage / cope with **stress**

stressful event/work place/environment/situation/life/journey/day/job

Complete the following sentences using an appropriate collocation:

1. I wish to __________ stress by surrounding myself with positive cues.
2. The stressful work _________ caused many people to leave the organisation.
3. _________ stress is a must to lead a balanced life.
4. They attended many workshops on stress ___________.
5. Jogging every day is a great stress ________.

Pronunciation

Word Stress

Stress is a significant aspect of the English language. Phonetically speaking, stress refers to the emphasis given to a particular syllable in a word. Stressing on the right part of the word can make your speech more intelligible. For instance, look at the words 'personal' and 'personnel'. In the word 'personal' the accent is on the first syllable and in the word 'personnel' the accent is on the third syllable.

The bar ˊ on the top of a syllable in a word indicates that that particular syllable is stressed (which is known as primary stress) and is more prominent than the other syllables. There might also be a bar below a syllable in a word (which is known as secondary stress). This indicates that this particular syllable is the next most prominent syllable.

Example: **ˌafter'noon**

Listening Exercise 3

Listen to the words below and repeat them, making sure that the part of the word in bold is stressed.

1.	a**lert**	11.	par**ti**cipate
2.	be**come**	12.	**peo**ple
3.	**chal**lenge	13.	pre**pare**
4.	**da**mage	14.	produc**ti**vity
5.	de**light**	15.	**qua**lity
6.	de**mand**	16.	re**move**
7.	ener**ge**tic	17.	res**pon**se
8.	**fo**cus	18.	**ser**vice
9.	**mo**dern	19.	**so**cial
10.	**mo**dify	20.	**val**ue

Sentence Stress

English is a stress-timed language, which means that you need to decide the words that are to be stressed in a sentence. In English, *content* words like nouns, adjectives, adverbs and main verbs are generally accented, whereas *structure* words like articles, pronouns, prepositions, conjunctions and auxiliaries are not.

Listening Exercise 4

Listen to the sentences below and repeat them, making sure that the parts of the words in bold are stressed.

1. Modern life is full of demands.
2. Stress has become a way of life.
3. Stress helps you stay focused, energetic, and alert.
4. The stress response helps you rise to meet challenges.
5. Stress can damage your productivity and quality of life.
6. Be prepared to modify your values.
7. Take delight in finding good things in other people.
8. Participate in social service activities.
9. Change your lifestyle by removing the causes of stress.
10. You must learn to celebrate your life.

Read aloud the sentences below to identify content words and structure words:

1. I always get the jitters the morning before an exam.
2. The collapse of the company has caused jitters in the financial markets.
3. He felt all jittery before the interview.
4. I get really jittery if I drink too much coffee.
5. The very thought of giving a speech in front of a large audience unnerves me.

Functional Grammar

Active and Passive Voice

Verb forms are said to be in the active voice when they express actions performed by the subject (the doer or agent). But when they express what the objects of those actions received, the verb forms are said to be in the passive voice. For example:

Active Voice :	Govind gave a presentation.
Passive Voice :	A presentation was given by Govind.
Active Voice :	Teachers must value the ideas of their students.
Passive Voice :	Students' ideas must be valued by their teachers.

The passive voice is generally used

1. When the action, but not the doer/agent is important.
   Example: Many interactive sessions were organized on stress management.
2. When the doer/agent is not known.
   Example: The reports have not been sent.

3. When the doer/agent is obvious.
   Example: Salaries have been hiked.
4. When you don't want to mention the doer/agent.
   Example: Steps must be taken to boost the morale of the employees.

Turn the following into the active voice:

1. The complete box must be used by employees.

   ____

2. Presentation tips must be learnt by students.

   ____

3. Stress management sessions must be arranged by the organization.

   ____

4. A friendly and co-operative atmosphere must be ensured by staff members.

   ____

5. Subordinates' work must be recognized by managers.

   ____

Expressing Suggestions: Pair Work

Writing Exercise 2

Read the following and suggest ways to manage stress:

- Swapna has to complete her project work in a week's time. She also has to take care of her younger brother because her mother is away on a business trip.
- Smitha thinks that some of her classmates are talking about her behind her back. She's so worried that it's affecting her studies.
- Murthy hasn't been sleeping well. He finds it hard to function effectively during the day. He's probably stressed at work.
- Vamshi is a workaholic. He has been neglecting his family for a very long time. His family is worried.
- Saritha has five important assignments to complete in three weeks' time. Saritha finds it difficult to finish all of them in time. Her class teacher is very strict about the work she assigns.

While offering your suggestions in the above situations, try to use active voice and not the passive voice.

For example, avoid the following:

Swapna's younger brother must be left with her relatives.

Present it in the following way instead:

Swapna must leave her younger brother with her relatives.

Direct and Indirect Speech

While writing, we may report a speech in two ways. When we quote the actual words of the speaker, it is said to be in **direct speech**.

For example:

"I have conveyed your message to Heather," Gina told Bob.

When one reports what the speaker said (that is, does not quote the exact words of the speaker), it is said to be in **indirect (or reported) speech.**

For example:

Mohan told Babu that he had conveyed his message to Raju.

(Here, it is a third person reporting what Mohan told Babu.)

Let us now see the differences between the two sentences:

No inverted commas (quotation marks) are used in the second sentence. The first and second person pronouns in the first statement are changed to third person pronouns. ('I' and 'your' are changed to 'she' and 'his' respectively.)The present perfect tense ('have conveyed') is changed to past perfect ('had conveyed').

The conjunction 'that' precedes the reported statement. Here are some more examples:

He said, "I like this movie."
He said that he liked that movie.
Father said, "I am going to Mumbai tomorrow."
Father said that he was going to Mumbai the next day.
Rohit said, "My sister cooks our breakfast."
Rohit said that his sister cooked their breakfast.
Radhika said, "I am not feeling well."
Radhika said that she was not feeling well.
Amit said, "I am staying in Jaipur for the week."
Amit said that he was staying in Jaipur for a week.

If the direct speech is in the form of a question, the reported statement is preceded by 'if'.

The stranger said, "Does anyone know the way?"
The stranger asked if anyone knew the way.

Words expressing nearness in time and place are changed into words expressing distance. Keep the following in mind:

now becomes **then**
this becomes **that**
these becomes **those**

here becomes **there**
thus becomes **so**
ago becomes **before**
today becomes **that day**
yesterday becomes **the day before/previous day**
tomorrow becomes **the next day**
last night becomes **the night before/previous night**
last week/month/year becomes **the week/month/year before**

OR

last week/month/year becomes **the previous week/month/year**

A. Rewrite the following sentences in the indirect speech.

1. Asif said, "I went to the market yesterday."
2. The doctor said, "I am very busy."
3. Mother said, "The baby is sleeping."
4. Mr Metha said, "I have bought a new car."
5. The principal said, "The school will remain closed tomorrow."
6. The villager said, "It was raining heavily last night."
7. The traveller said, "I am going to sit here and take some rest."
8. Mary said, "The children are playing in the park."
9. The teacher said, "Have you ever seen a balloon rising in the sky?"

Now, examine the following sentences:

She said to me, "I have never seen such a lazy girl as you."
She told me that she had never seen such a lazy girl as I.
The teacher said to the boy, "I know you and your father."
The teacher told the boy that she knew him and his father.
Father said to Mother, "I received some letters from Kanpur."
Father told Mother that he had received letters from Kanpur.
Mrs Rao said to her son, "When will you come home?"
Mrs Rao asked her son when he would come home.

When you want to mention the person to whom the speech is addressed, use 'told' or 'said to'; never use 'to' with 'told'.

B. Rewrite the following sentences in the indirect speech.

1. The manager said to me, "You have to go to Chennai for one week."
2. The boy said to his mother, "I am very hungry."
3. The cunning fox said to the crow, "You sing so well."
4. Aastha said to Rachit, "I have misplaced my expensive pen case."
5. The robber said to the policemen, "We were very frightened when we heard the loud explosion."
6. Hamid said, "I have football practice after school today."

Look at these sentences:

The teacher said to the students, "The earth is round."

The teacher told the students that the earth is round.

Grandfather said to Mohit, "Honesty is the best policy."

Grandfather told Mohit that honesty is the best policy.

The above sentences express universal truths. Thus, we do not change is to 'was', that is, we do not change the tense.

C. Rewrite the following sentences in the indirect speech.

1. Mrs Jones said to the students, "The sun rises in the east."
2. He said, "I am glad to be here this evening."
3. Grandmother said to me, "I have told you not to come home so late in the evening."

Conversion of indirect speech into direct speech

Examine the following sentences. Notice how the sentences are punctuated when they are re-written in direct speech.

The boy told his friend that he would meet him the next day outside the gym.

The boy said to his friend, "I will meet you tomorrow outside the gym."

The doctor told the patient that if he did not take the medicine regularly, he would not get well.

The doctor said to the patient, "If you do not take the medicine regularly, you will not get well."

D. Rewrite the following sentences in direct speech.

1. The thief confessed that he was guilty.
2. The principal told me that I was wrong and would be fined.
3. Ankit told the teacher that he had forgotten to bring his book.
4. They told me that I deserved their thanks for all I had done for them.
5. The soldiers told their officer that they would fight the enemy till their last breath.
6. The tourists told the guide that they were extremely delighted to see all the beautiful monuments.
7. The children asked the man if he had the new chocolate ice cream that had been introduced recently.
8. Mrs Reddy told mother that her son was leaving for the USA the next day.

Spelling

Look at the sets of words below and circle the word with the correct spelling. Check your answers with the other members of your team. If you need to, use a good dictionary to find the correct spelling.

1.	anxiety	anxety	anxeity	anxietty
2.	workhalic	workaholic	workholic	workohalic
3.	inferiority	infferiority	inferoirity	inferiorrity
4.	parspective	perspictive	perspectave	perspective
5.	charracteristic	characterristic	charactaristic	characteristic
6.	managment	manegement	management	menagement
7.	atmosphere	atmasphere	atmmosphere	atmospher
8.	assignment	asignment	assinment	assignmant
9.	niglect	negglect	neglact	neglect
10.	parsuade	persade	perssuade	persuade

6 A New Beginning

In this unit

Reading
"A New Beginning": Speech by Barack Obama

Structural Grammar
Sentence Transformation

Listening
Interpersonal Communication

Speaking
Asking for Information Politely

Writing
Resume Writing
Writing the Job Application Letter or Cover Letter

Pronunciation
Phonemic Symbols and Sounds

Vocabulary
Ways of Speaking

Functional Grammar
Modal Verbs

Spelling

Barack Hussein Obama is the 44th President of the United States of America, and the first African American to hold the office. On the fourth of June, 2009, President Obama made a speech at Cairo University in which he appealed for greater understanding between the United States of America and the Muslim World. An extract from his speech is reproduced here.

Reading

"A New Beginning": Speech by Barack Obama

I have come here to seek a new beginning between the United States and Muslims around the world; one based upon mutual interest and mutual respect; and one based upon the truth that America and Islam are not exclusive, and need not be in competition. Instead, they overlap, and share common principles—principles of justice and progress; tolerance and the dignity of all human beings.

I do so recognizing that change cannot happen overnight. No single speech can eradicate years of mistrust, nor can I answer in the time that I have all the complex questions that brought us to this point. But I am convinced that in order to move forward, we must say openly the things we hold in our hearts, and that too often are said only behind closed doors. There must be a sustained effort to listen to each other; to learn from each other; to respect one another; and to seek common ground. As the Holy Koran tells us, "Be conscious of God and speak always the truth." That is what I will try to do—to speak the truth as best I can, humbled by the task before us, and firm in my belief that the interests we share as human beings are far more powerful than the forces that drive us apart.

Part of this conviction is rooted in my own experience. I am a Christian, but my father came from a Kenyan family that includes generations of Muslims. As a boy, I spent several years in Indonesia and heard the call of the azaan at the break of dawn and the fall of dusk. As a young man, I worked in Chicago communities where many found dignity and peace in their Muslim faith.

As a student of history, I also know civilization's debt to Islam. It was Islam—at places like Al-Azhar University—that carried the light of learning through so many centuries, paving the way for Europe's Renaissance and Enlightenment. It was innovation in Muslim communities that developed the order of algebra; our magnetic compass and tools of navigation; our mastery of pens and printing; our understanding of how disease spreads and how it can be healed. Islamic culture has given us majestic arches and soaring spires; timeless poetry and cherished music; elegant **calligraphy** and places of peaceful **contemplation**. And throughout history, Islam has demonstrated through words and deeds the possibilities of religious tolerance and racial equality.

calligraphy
decorative handwriting, typically found in books of the islamic world or on islamic architecture

contemplation
to be engaged in deep thought

I know, too, that Islam has always been a part of America's story. The first nation to recognize my country was Morocco. In signing the Treaty of Tripoli in 1796, our second President John Adams wrote, "The United States has in itself no character of enmity against the laws, religion or tranquility of Muslims." And since our founding, American Muslims have enriched the United States. They have fought in our wars, served in government, stood for civil rights, started businesses, taught at

our Universities, excelled in our sports arenas, won Nobel Prizes, built our tallest building, and lit the Olympic Torch. And when the first Muslim-American was recently elected to Congress, he took the oath to defend our Constitution using the same Holy Koran that one of our Founding Fathers—Thomas Jefferson—kept in his personal library.

So I have known Islam on three continents before coming to the region where it was first revealed. That experience guides my conviction that partnership between America and Islam must be based on what Islam is, not what it isn't. And I consider it part of my responsibility as President of the United States to fight against negative **stereotype**s of Islam wherever they appear.

stereotype
a common image of an individual or a community

But, that same principle must apply to Muslim perceptions of America. Just as Muslims do not fit a crude stereotype, America is not the crude stereotype of a self-interested empire. The United States has been one of the greatest sources of progress that the world has ever known. We were born out of revolution against an empire. We were founded upon the ideal that all are created equal, and we have shed blood and struggled for centuries to give meaning to those words—within our borders, and around the world. We are shaped by every culture, drawn from every end of the Earth, and dedicated to a simple concept: *E pluribus unum*: "Out of many, one."

Much has been made of the fact that an African-American with the name Barack Hussein Obama could be elected President. But my personal story is not so unique. The dream of opportunity for all people has not come true for everyone in America, but its promise exists for all who come to our shores—that includes nearly seven million American Muslims in our country today who enjoy incomes and education that are higher than average.

'Moreover, freedom in America is indivisible from the freedom to practice one's religion. That is why there is a mosque in every state of our union, and over 1,200 mosques within our borders. That is why the U.S. government has gone to court to protect the right of women and girls to wear the hijab, and to punish those who would deny it.

So let there be no doubt: Islam is a part of America. And I believe that America holds within her the truth that regardless of race, religion, or station in life, all of us share common aspirations—to live in peace and security; to get an education and to work with dignity; to love our families, our communities, and our God. These things we share. This is the hope of all humanity.

Of course, recognizing our common humanity is only the beginning of our task. Words alone cannot meet the needs of our people. These needs will be met only if we act boldly in the years ahead; and if we understand that the challenges we face are shared, and our failure to meet them will hurt us all.

For we have learned from recent experience that when a financial system weakens in one country, prosperity is hurt everywhere. When a new flu infects one human being, all are at risk.

slaughter
kill mercilessly. the word is associated with butchers

When one nation pursues a nuclear weapon, the risk of nuclear attack rises for all nations. When violent extremists operate in one stretch of mountains, people are endangered across an ocean. And when innocents in Bosnia and Darfur are **slaughtered**, that is a stain on our collective conscience. That is what it means to share this world in the 21st century. That is the responsibility we have to one another as human beings.

This is a difficult responsibility to embrace. For human history has often been a record of nations and tribes subjugating one another to serve their own interests. Yet in this new age, such attitudes are self-defeating. Given our interdependence, any world order that elevates one nation or group of people over another will inevitably fail. So whatever we think of the past, we must not be prisoners of it. Our problems must be dealt with through partnership; progress must be shared.

All of us share this world for but a brief moment in time. The question is whether we spend that time focused on what pushes us apart, or whether we commit ourselves to an effort—a sustained effort—to find common ground, to focus on the future we seek for our children, and to respect the dignity of all human beings.

'It is easier to start wars than to end them. It is easier to blame others than to look inward; to see what is different about someone than to find the things we share. But, we should choose the right path, not just the easy path. There is also one rule that lies at the heart of every religion—that we do unto others as we would have them do unto us. This truth **transcends** nations and peoples—a belief that isn't new; that isn't black or white or brown; that isn't Christian, or Muslim or Jew. It's a belief that pulsed in the cradle of civilization, and that still beats in the heart of billions. It's a faith in other people, and it's what brought me here today.

transcend
to go beyond a limit or range of thought or belief

We have the power to make the world we seek, but only if we have the courage to make a new beginning, keeping in mind what has been written.

The Holy Koran tells us, "O mankind! We have created you male and a female; and we have made you into nations and tribes so that you may know one another."

The Talmud tells us: "The whole of the Torah is for the purpose of promoting peace."

The Holy Bible tells us, "Blessed are the peacemakers, for they shall be called sons of God."

The people of the world can live together in peace. We know that is God's vision. Now, that must be our work here on Earth. Thank you. And may God's peace be upon you.

Comprehension

1. What, according to President Obama, are the common principles of America and Islam?
2. How has Islam been a part of President Obama's childhood?
3. What have been the contributions of Islam to Western civilization?
4. 'I know, too, that Islam has always been a part of America's story'—read the above passage carefully to substantiate President Obama's statement.
5. What is the stereotype of America that President Obama objects to? How does he refute the stereotype?

Think and Write

President Obama's speech employs a balanced use of both short and long sentences: "Words alone cannot meet the needs of our people. These needs will be met only if we act boldly in the years ahead; and if we understand that the challenges we face are shared, and our failure to meet them will hurt us all." He uses simple words succinctly, making them more effective: "All of us share this world for but a brief moment in time." He does not say, "All humans are mortal and the world is transient and transience is a great leveler". Repetition has been used to create rhythm and balance: "It is easier to start wars than to end them. It is easier to blame others than to look inward; to see what is different about someone than to find the things we share. But, we should choose the right path, not just the easy path."

Try writing a similar speech responding to the one here.

Structural Grammar

Convert the following sentences as instructed:

1. The Holy Koran tells us, "O mankind! We have created you male and a female; and we have made you into nations and tribes so that you may know one another." **(Change to reported speech)**
2. Much has been made of the fact that an African-American with the name Barack Hussein Obama could be elected President. **(Change to the active voice)**
3. But, we should choose the right path, not just the easy path. **(Change to passive voice)**.
4. It is easier to start wars than to end them. **(Rewrite using *not*)**
5. The people of the world can live together in peace. We know that is God's vision. **(Join the two sentences without using *and*)**

Listening

Listening Exercise 1

Listen to the dialogue on interpersonal communication between an teacher and her student, and then answer the following questions:

1. What is interpersonal communication?

   ____
   ____
   ____

2. What are the functions of interpersonal communication?

   ____
   ____
   ____

3. What needs to be done to achieve interpersonal effectiveness?

   ____
   ____
   ____

4. What are some of the conversation techniques?

   ____
   ____
   ____

Listening Exercise 2

Listen to the presentation on effective listening skills, and then answer the following questions:

1. How important is listening as a skill?

   ____

   ____

   ____

2. With what efficiency do people tend to listen?

   ____

   ____

   ____

3. What is the difference between listening and hearing?

   ____

   ____

   ____

4. How important are nonverbal cues in listening?

   ____

   ____

   ____

5. Why should a listener empathize with the speaker?

   ____

   ____

   ____

Speaking

Pair Work: Asking for Information Politely

Speaking Exercise 1

Collect information about your partner for the topics below using questions that begin with 'can', 'could', 'would', etc. Share the information you've gathered with the class.

Example: Could I know what your favourite book is?

1. Favourite actor
2. Favourite actress
3. Favourite author
4. Favourite book
5. Favourite colour
6. Favourite day of the week
7. Favourite holiday spot
8. Favourite movie
9. Role model
10. Goals in life

My partner's profile

____

____

____

Speaking Exercise 2

The Person I Admire the Most

Give a speech about the person you admire the most, focusing specifically on the following:

- How he or she uses language
- How effective is he or she as a communicator
- How well is he or she listens
- How powerful he or she is nonverbally
- How he or she relates himself or herself with others

Use the space below to draft your speech.

____

____

____

Writing

Resume Writing

Your resume (also called bio-data or curriculum vitae) is a necessary annexure to any job application. It is a document that lists the personal details, objectives and achievements of a person in a simple format. There is, as such, no standard format for a resume. The most important thing to remember while drafting a resume is the purpose of the resume. Therefore, apart from being informative, the arrangement of data in a resume should make document look focused and convincing.

Resume Writing Tips

- Use headings for separate sections of the resume
- Use phrases in point form rather than full sentences
- Refer first to those aspects that have a direct relationship with the application that you are preparing
- Be positive in the choice of terms
- Arrange your most impressive achievements first

The resume could be thematically arranged under different headings or be chronological, that is, the entries could be organized by date. In a chronological arrangement, you might want to use reverse chronology, that is, place the most recent entries first.

Headings

Possible headings for a resume for job applications are:

- Name
- Contact information
- Statement of professional objectives
- Work experience
- Academic and professional qualifications
- Extra-curricular activities
- References

Statement of Professional Objectives

Mention your career objective in a short statement based on your skills and competencies. Note that the next section depends on whether you have more points under work experience or under educational qualifications. Whichever has greater significance comes next.

Work Experience

List your work experience, starting with your current job. Mention the name of the organization, the position held, the nature of the post, your work responsibilities, the period of work, and, optionally, the salary.

Academic and Professional Qualifications

Arrange your academic qualifications and professional qualifications separately, again with the most recent ones coming first. You should mention the name of the course, the examination passed, and year of passing, the institution and the results. Any special distinction that you have achieved should be pointed out.

Extra-Curricular Activities

Under this heading, list all those activities and achievements that project you as a person with a range of interests. Remember to include awards from school and college, the positions you held, and the social service initiatives you took.

References

Do not give too many references. Two or three should suffice. You should seek the prior consent of your references before you actually give their names. Provide their postal and e-mail addresses, telephone numbers, etc., so that they can be easily contacted. Try to provide a variety of referees from your teachers and supervisors in the workplace. Do not include relatives.

RESUME TEMPLATES

Below is a simple resume template that you can follow. You can draft slight variations of it to make it stand out among the others.

Template 1

Name: ____________________

Contact Information: ____________________

____

Objectives: ____________________

____

Work Experience: ____________________

____

Extra-Curricular Activities: ____________________

____

References: ____________________

____

Signature: ____________________

Here is another resume template where the academic qualifications follow the description of work experience. Remember that it is very important to detail your work experience, so that your employer has a clear idea of what kind of work you actually do. It will help them to place you better in their organization.

Template 2

Name: ____________________

Address: ____________________

____

Phone: ____________________

Email: ____________________

Career Objectives: ____________________

____

____

Job Experience (*the most recent one should come first*)

1. **Job Title:** __________ **Dates:** ______ **(Month/Year)**

   Employer: __________

   Responsibilities:

   ____

   ____

   ____

2. **Job Title:** __________ **Dates:** ______ **(Month/Year)**

   Employer: __________

   Responsibilities:

   ____

   ____

   ____

Education (*the most recent one should come first*)

Degree: ____________ Date: ______ (Month/Year)

Degree: ____________ Date: ______ (Month/Year)

Degree: ____________ Date: ______ (Month/Year)

Degree: ____________ Date: ______ (Month/Year)

Training and Certification:

Certificate: ____________ Date: ______ (Month/Year)

Certificate: ____________ Date: ______ (Month/Year)

Publication(s):

Title: ____________

Source: ____________

Date: ____________

Hobbies: ______________________________________

____

References: ______________________________________

Writing the Job Application Letter or Cover Letter

You will need to send a covering letter along with the resume. The purpose of a over letter is to arouse the interest of your prospective employers, and to increase the chance that they will call you for an interview. See unit 5 for formats of this letter.

Sections of a Job Application Letter

The following are the three sections of a job application letter

- Opening
- Middle paragraphs
- Closing

Opening

In the opening part, mention how you learnt about this job opportunity. Write two or three sentences summarizing your most outstanding qualifications related to the job you are seeking.

Middle Paragraph

- Education
- Work experience
- Personal details like interests, activities, qualities.

Education

Mention how your overall education has prepared you for the work you are seeking. Also, talk about your specialization along with an in-depth knowledge of the field. Give details of any extra-educational qualifications you have in addition to the course you graduated in. State any other courses that complement your knowledge in the relevant areas.

Work Experience

Here, you can state the following:

- How you gained practical experience in addition to your education
- How you adapted to different working environments
- Things you have accomplished in any of the tasks assigned to you in your previous jobs
- How well you work in a group towards the fulfilment of a shared goal
- How you can prove your sustained interest in your chosen field
- Things that show your determination, initiative, integrity, etc.

Closing Paragraph

Give details of how and when you can be reached (by phone, fax, email, etc.). End the paragraph with a sentence along the lines of "I look forward to hearing from you".

Other Essentials of a Cover Letter

- The cover letter should be concise and to the point, and usually no longer than one page.
- It should be addressed formally and to the most appropriate person in the organization.
- The letter should be formatted well, with proper spacing.
- Leave about six or seven lines blank at the top of the page.
- If you know who should be contacted, mention the person's name.
- Add your contact details on the cover letter.
- Mention that you have enclosed your resume.
- Sign and date your letter.

It is always best to go through the letter a few times before making the final draft.

Writing Exercise 1

Create a resume for yourself, keeping in mind all that you have learnt and following an appropriate format.

Draft an application letter in response to an advertisement. From the weekly employment supplement of the newspaper, or from the internet, collect five advertisements that are related to the kind of job you are interested in. Write an application letter for these positions.

Pronunciation

Phonemic Symbols and Sounds

Learn the following phonemic symbols to help you learn the correct pronunciation of English words.

Listening Exercise 3

Listen to the following words and repeat:

Vowel sounds

Symbol/Sound	**Keyword**		
/ə/	about	/iː/	eat
/ɑː/	ask	/ʊ/	pull
/ɪ/	it	/uː/	pool

Symbol/Sound	Keyword		
/e/	pen	/aɪ/	ice
/æ/	pat	/ɔɪ/	boy
/ʌ/	cut	/ɪə/	dear
/ɜː/	girl	/eə/	fair
/ɒ/	cot	/ʊə/	poor
/ɔː/	caught	/aʊ/	out
/eɪ/	say	/əʊ/	go

Consonant sounds

/p/	pack	/m/	meet
/b/	back	/n/	neat
/t/	ten	/ŋ/	bank
/d/	den	/h/	hat
/tʃ/	cheap	/s/	seat
/dʒ/	jeep	/z/	zoo
/k/	kit	/ʃ/	ship
/g/	get	/ʒ/	pleasure
/f/	fan	/r/	read
/v/	van	/l/	lead
/θ/	thin	/j/	yet
/ð/	then	/w/	wet

Listening Exercise 4

Pronunciation of '-ed' and '-es'

Study the pronunciation of words that end in '-ed' and '-es'.

Listen to the words below:

booked	bagged	batted
books	bags	buses

You might have noticed that in the word 'booked' the letters 'ed' are pronounced as /t/, in the word 'bagged' the letters 'ed' are pronounced as /d/, and in the word 'batted' the letters 'ed' are pronounced as /ɪd/. And in the word 'books' the letter 's' is pronounced as /s/, in the word 'bags' the letter 's' is pronounced as /z/ and in the word 'buses' the letters 'es' are pronounced as /ɪz/.

The variation in pronunciation of '-ed' and '-es' is due to the phonetic environment in which they occur, i.e., whether they come after voiced or voiceless sounds. In English, the voiceless sounds are /p/, /t/, /k/, /f/, /θ/, /s/, /ʃ/, /h/and /tʃ/ and the voiced sounds are the rest of the consonant sounds and all the vowel sounds.

Here are the three rules for pronunciation of '-ed':

1) /t/ after voiceless sounds excepting /t/.

Examples:

clapped	/klæpt/
missed	/mɪst/
crushed	/krʌʃt/
reached	/ri:tʃt/

2) /d/ after voiced sounds excepting /d/.

Examples:

dragged	/drægd/	fried	/fraɪd/
cleaned	/kli:nd/	summed	/sʌmd/
cured	/kjuəd/	loved	/lʌvd/
curbed	/kɜ:bd		

3) /Id/ after /t/ and /d/.

Examples:

painted	/peɪntɪd/	wanted	/wɔ:ntɪd
sounded	/saʊndɪd/	grounded	/graʊndɪd/

Pronunciation of '-s/-es'

Here are the three rules for pronunciation of '-s/-es':

1) /s/ after voiceless sounds excepting /s/, /ʃ/ and /tʃ/

Examples:

caps	/kæps/	writes	/raɪts/
laughs	/lɑ:fs/	picks	/pɪks/
hits	/hɪts/	pats	/pæts/

2) /z/ after voiced sounds excepting /z/, /ʒ/ and /dʒ/

Examples:

rags	/rægz/	toys	/tɔɪz/
friends	/frendz/	ends	/endz/
dreams	/dri:mz/	legs	/legz/
cleans	/kli:nz/	fans	/fænz/

3) /ɪz/ after /s/, /ʃ/, /tʃ /, /z/, /ʒ / and / dʒ/

Examples:

places /pleɪsɪz/

crushes /krʌʃɪz/

searches /sɜ:tʃɪz/

Note that the words ending in '-ed' that function as adjectives are pronounced as /ɪd/. For instance, when the word 'blessed' is used as verb it is pronounced as /blest/ but when it is used as an adjective it is pronounced as /blesɪd/.

Listening Exercise 5

Listen to the following sentences and say them aloud, making sure that you pronounce the parts of the words in bold correctly.

1. Vandana visit**ed** many plac**es**.
2. She work**ed** in a reput**ed** organization.
3. They've demolish**ed** many buildings.
4. They cleaned some lak**es** and rivers.
5. We watch**ed** many movi**es**.

Vocabulary

Ways of speaking

Match the words under 'A' with their meanings under 'B'.

'A'	'B'
1. announce	a) to cry out loudly, in fear, pain or excitement
2. argue	b) to give a formal talk to a group of people
3. assert	c) to give unwanted advice
4. babble	d) to interrupt a conversation or discussion
5. bellow	e) to make a continuous, low sound
6. blurt out	f) to make a loud, deep sound
7. butt in	g) to make a low, rough noise
8. chat	h) to make something clear, giving details
9. clarify	i) to make something known
10. croak	j) to say or write something clearly and carefully

(Continued)

(Continued)

11. discuss	k) to say quickly and in a confused way
12. gossip	l) to say something in a quiet, angry way
13. grunt	m) to say something suddenly and without thinking
14. hiss	n) to say that something is certainly true
15. hum	o) to speak about something quickly, giving little detail
16. lecture	p) to speak angrily
17. mention	q) to speak in a high-pitched voice
18. murmur	r) to speak in a soft, quiet voice that is difficult to hear clearly
19. narrate	s) to speak while trembling out of nervousness or distress
20. preach	t) to speak unclearly, without separating the words correctly
21. quaver	u) to speak with a rough voice
22. slur	v) to speak with pauses and repeating the same sound or syllable
23. squeak	w) to talk about a subject with someone
24. stammer	x) to talk about other people's private lives
25. state	y) to talk to someone in a friendly, informal way
26. yell	z) to tell a story

Functional Grammar

Modal Verbs

You use words like 'can', 'could', 'will', 'would', 'may', 'might', 'shall' and 'should' to talk about different functions of language such as asking for information making and offers, requests, or suggestions. These words are referred to as modal verbs.

Can is used to express ability, possibility, generalization, etc.

1. I **can** swim really well. (ability)
2. I **can** practise more on Sundays. (possibility)
3. Parking vehicles here **can** be risky. (generalization about what is true all the time)

Use 'can' and write a sentence that indicates the following:

1. ability / inability

___

2. possibility

___

3. generalization about what is true all the time

___

Could is used to express suggestion, possibility, ability, etc.

1. He **could** climb very tall trees in his younger days. (past ability)
2. He **could** have revealed the secret. (possibility)
3. I **can't** sing a song. (present ability)
4. You **could** go out for a walk in the evenings. (suggestion)

Use 'could' and write a sentence that indicates the following:

1. guess

___

2. past ability / inability

___

3. present ability / inability

___

May is used to express possibility, uncertainty and wishes, and to seek or give permission.

1. I **may** go to Goa next Monday. (possibility)
2. **May** you have a bright career! (wish)
3. I **may** not complete my project before the deadline. (doubt/uncertainty)
4. **May** I leave now? (seeking permission)
5. You **may** go out now. (giving permission)

Note: 'Can' is often used instead of 'may' while making requests.

Use 'may' and write a sentence that indicates the following:

1. doubt

___

2. giving permission

___

3. possibility

___

4. seeking permission

___

5. wish

___

Might is used to express possibility, suggestion, requests, offers, etc.

1. It **might** rain heavily. (possibility)
2. You **might** try using some lotion. (suggestion)
3. **Might** I come with you? (request)
4. I **might** help you here if you like. (offer)

Use 'might' and write a sentence that indicates the following:

1. possibility

   ____
2. suggestion

   ____
3. request

   ____
4. offer

   ____

Will is used to express a promise, willingness, a command, insistence, capacity, intention, a prediction, etc.

1. I **will** not reveal the secret. (promise)
2. India **will** become a superpower. (prediction)
3. This hull **will** not withstand the pressure. (capacity)
4. We **will** go to Osman Sagar on a picnic. (intention)
5. **Will** you close the window for me, please? (request)
6. You **will** not go out to play today. (command)

Use 'will' and write a sentence that indicates the following:

1. capacity

   ____
2. command

   ____
3. intention

   ____
4. obligation

   ____
5. offer

   ____
6. prediction

   ____
7. request

   ____

Would is used to express determination, intention, habitual action, willingness, futurity, a request, a wish, etc.

1. **Would** you please get that for me? (request)
2. Every morning he **would** sell newspapers. (habitual action)
3. I **would** like to join your party. (wish)
4. She said she **would** serve the nation. (intention)

Use 'will' to write a sentence that indicates the following:

1. express a wish
______
2. habitual action
______
3. a request
______
4. intention/desire
______

Shall is used to express intention, a command, a threat, a promise, compulsion, determination, certainty, the future, etc.

1. **Shall** we dance? (suggestion)
2. We **shall** form a new party. (intention)
3. You **shall** not smoke here. (command)
4. **Shall** we go out and have lunch? (request)
5. We **shall** fight till the end. (determination)
6. I **shall** visit you tomorrow. (future)

Use 'shall' and write a sentence that indicates the following:

1. a suggestion
______
2. a command
______
3. intention
______
4. a request
______
5. determination
______
6. the future
______

Should is used to express obligation, instruction, duty, opinion, advice, the future, purpose, suggestion, etc.

1. You **should** serve your country. (obligation)
2. You **should** complete your work this evening. (instruction)
3. Everyone **should** take regular exercise. (advice)
4. **Should** I accept this offer? (opinion)
5. He **should** discover the secret anytime. (expectation)
6. **Shouldn't** you be in class now? (surprise)

Use 'should' and write a sentence that indicates the following:

1. obligation ______________________________
2. instruction ______________________________
3. advice ______________________________
4. opinion ______________________________
5. expectation ______________________________
6. surprise ______________________________

Must is used to express obligation, prohibition, necessity, duty, certainty, probability, etc.

1. I **must** get up early in the morning. (obligation)
2. This **must** be the right way to do this. (certainty)
3. We **mustn't** play here. (prohibition)
4. Everyone **must** submit their résumés in two days. (strong recommendation)

Use 'must' and write sentences that indicate the following:

1. obligation ______________________________
2. certainty ______________________________
3. prohibition ______________________________
4. strong recommendation ______________________________

Spelling

Look at the sets of words below and circle the word with the correct spelling. Check your answers with the other members of your team. If you need to, use a good dictionary to find the correct spelling.

1.	recomendation	recammendation	recommendation	recommendetion
2.	questionaire	questionnaire	questionniare	quesstionnaire
3.	permmission	permision	permmission	permission
4.	certainity	cartainty	certtainty	certainty
5.	prohibition	prahibition	prohibission	prohibision
6.	privilige	privelege	previlege	privilege
7.	disapear	dissappear	disapper	disappear
8.	disclosare	disclosure	dissclosure	disclosur
9.	higemony	heggemony	hegemany	hegemony
10.	disuasion	dissuasion	dissuassion	disuassion

7

Perilous Plastic Bags

In this unit

Reading
Perilous Plastic Bags

Structural Grammar
Prefixes and Suffixes

Listening
A Conversation on Time Management

Speaking
Dealing with Time Robbers

Writing
Report Writing

Pronunciation
Contractions

Vocabulary
A Crossword Puzzle

Functional Grammar
Articles
Prepositions

Spelling

Being inexpensive, easy to manufacture, flexible and durable, it is no wonder that plastics are used in an enormous range of products, invading almost every facet of life in the 21st century. However, the same durability that makes plastics so popular has now made them a threat to the environment and to our lives. To know more about the threat caused by just one of the many everyday uses of plastic, read this report.

Reading

Perilous Plastic Bags

Hanging from the branches, flying in the air, racing along with the vehicles on the road are plastic bags. This wonder material of the 20th century has **invaded** every aspect of our lives; it is everywhere, messing up the streets and parks, **clogging** up the drains and gutters. These plastic bags, or shoppers, as they are commonly called, are available in all sizes, shapes and colours, and because of their light weight, flexibility and low cost they are used and cast off freely.

Today people from all walks of life use plastic bags mainly because of their easy availability and convenience. Their use is so widespread that it is a wonder how people ever managed to do anything without them. There are a variety of bags available, and they are put to different uses. The grocer packs most of the food into clean, transparent plastic bags. Other items like clothes, toys, shoes, electric items and magazines are pre-packed in plastic bags before being sold. Apart from making it convenient for the consumer to buy them, these pre-weighed and clean packages help save time and energy for the buyer.

On the home front, students and office goers prefer to pack lunches in plastic bags, saving the effort of carrying and washing lunch boxes. Housemaids use these bags to carry food from their places of work to their home. Deep freezers are also stocked with food stored in plastic bags.

The plastic carry bags and garbage bags too have become an **indispensable** part of our lives. Garbage packed in a plastic bag keeps our homes free from flies and other insects, while a shopping spree becomes much more convenient when these disposable plastic bags are around to carry all the purchased items. Manufacturers too find these bags very effective to **advertise** their products.

This is one side of the story. Looking at the other side—what happens when we are through with these bags? How do we get rid of them? We throw them out, but where do they go? How are they disposed of? After coming into our homes, they are either thrown in garbage bins or left lying around till they are carried away by the wind. These plastic bags can be seen **dangling** from trees, electric wires, poles and balconies of houses. Wherever they land, they create an **eyesore**, and cleaning up the mess becomes a **cumbersome** task.

About 10 million plastic bags are thrown away every day as waste. These bags cause blockages in the drainage and the sewage system of the city, causing waterlogging, germination of bacterial and water-borne diseases, and the spread of mosquitoes. There are about 80 diseases caused by water-borne germs, and only one piece of plastic is enough to block a drain.

invade
to enter using force in order to take control

clog
to get blocked by something

indispensable
too important to be without

advertise
to publicize

dangling
to hang or swing freely

eyesore
an object that is unpleasant to look at

cumbersome
large and heavy

According to researchers, plastic degrades slowly. It could take anywhere from twenty to a thousand years. All plastics sooner or later break down into small pieces, leaving behind plastic-chunks or plastic-dust. These chunks and dust are not biodegradable, as their molecular structure is too large for micro-organisms to swallow. This characteristic of plastic causes serious environmental and health problems.

The International Rice Research Institute has found that plastic bags have harmful effects on the soil, water and air. In fields, when these plastic bags are deposited in high quantities, they cause soil **infertility**. The accumulation of plastic prevents sunlight from entering the soil, thus destroying the beneficial bacteria that are so necessary for soil fertility. The acidic combination present in plastic, after a period of time, disturbs the chemical formula of the soil, again causing loss of fertility. Since the plastic bags are picked up from the garbage and recycled, they tend to retain a lot of bacteria that are difficult to destroy, which in turn contaminates the food the bag will hold, causing illnesses. The burning of plastic in temperatures less than 800 degrees Celsius in an open space creates noxious fumes such as hydrogen cyanide and other poisonous gases that cause air pollution, resulting in skin and respiratory problems, and also certain kinds of cancer. Plastic wastes have disastrous effects on the species living underwater when dumped in or thrown into rivers, ponds or the sea, and a lot of marine life is lost due to this.

infertile
not able to produce crops

Hazards on Land

Plastic waste blocks drains and gutters, stopping the flow of rainwater and sewage, causing an overflow that becomes the breeding ground for germs and bacteria. The toxic smoke produced while burning plastic kills thousands each year. Workers and people living near a plastic or resin factory are prone to certain kinds of cancer and birth defects. Plastic bags that land on agricultural land retard the growth of crops. Plastic waste that lies on the soil blocks the passage of oxygen, causing soil infertility. Domestic animals like cows and goats often die after swallowing bits of plastic that get mingled in the grass they eat.

Hazards in the Sea

There are approximately 46,000 pieces of plastic floating in each square mile in coastal areas. More than one million sea birds and approximately 100,000 sea mammals die each year after **ingesting** or becoming **entangled** in plastic debris. Turtles, dolphins and other such marine creatures often mistake small plastic bags for jellyfish, and develop intestinal blockades after eating them, which often lead to their death. It is surprising that in a world full of plastic users, very few are aware of the harmful effects of plastic even though environmentalists have been busy trying to create awareness of the hazards of plastic. Schools and colleges are educating the students about plastic hazards. Many countries have banned the use of plastic bags and many are in the process of doing so. Despite all

ingest
to swallow anything

entangle
to get caught or twisted in something

this, the menace of plastic bags seems to be ever increasing. The statistics listed below will show the amount of plastics we use and discard.

- Twelve million plastic bags are handed out to shoppers in Britain every year.
- Ten million plastic bags are disposed of by Bangladeshi nationals every year.
- Six billion plastic bags are thrown away by Australians every minute.
- The use of plastic in India has more than doubled in the last 20 years.
- It has increased from 1.8 million tons to about 5 million tons since 1995–96.

These statistics are from only a few countries. If we add up the plastics used all over the world the amount of plastic used and discarded will be enormous. Since plastics' non-biodegradability is creating serious environmental and health problems, something should be done about it.

Do we have to wait for a ban on use of plastics to stop using them? Why don't we take the initiative, and make a conscious effort to stop using plastic bags? If we all do our bit to keep our environment clean and healthy, we will leave a clean and healthy environment for the next generation.

Comprehension

1. Why have plastic carry bags become very important in human lives?
2. Explain the harmful effects of plastic bags on soil.
3. What are the effects of plastic bags on wildlife?
4. What are the hazards of plastic bags floating in the sea?
5. Why should we not burn plastic bags?

Structural Grammar

Prefixes and Suffixes

The meaning of the word 'biodegradable' is 'able to decay naturally and in a way that is not harmful'. Now, working in pairs, write as many words as you can with 'bio-' as a prefix as well as their meanings. Check with other classmates and list all the words with 'bio-' as prefix. The word 'dentist' ends with the suffix '-ist'. Write as many words that end with the prefix '-ist' as you can think of.

bio ____________ ____________ ist
bio ____________ ____________ ist
bio ____________ ____________ ist
bio ____________ ____________ ist
bio ____________ ____________ ist
bio ____________ ____________ ist
bio ____________ ____________ ist
bio ____________ ____________ ist
bio ____________ ____________ ist
bio ____________ ____________ ist

Think and Write

You have seen a report on the environment in Unit 2. The report in this unit also makes use of simple language and statistics to support its argument. The tone is more informal, and appeals more directly to the reader. A report can be more persuasive if it moves the reader to sympathy, disgust, outrage, etc. However, it is important to strike a balance—you must interest readers, but not rouse their emotions to the point that they will stop reading in disgust, or stop taking you seriously. Note also how the above report refers to matters of everyday life before moving on to matters more distant to the reader. This has the effect of directly involving the reader in the argument.

Write a report on a topic that you feel is important but is often ignored.

Listening

A Conversation on Time Management

Listening Exercise 1

1. What is time management?

2. How important is it to manage one's time?

3. What should one do to manage one's time effectively?

4. What is the importance of the Pareto principle?

5. What is the POSEC method?

Speaking

Dealing with Time Robbers

Speaking Exercise 1

Listen to the talk on time management and then, in pairs, answer the questions below. Make a list of time robbers and talk about ways to deal with each of the time robbers you've identified.

Time robbers	Ways of dealing with time robbers

Speaking Exercise 2

Discuss with your team members and identify the common time management tools the team uses. Talk about advantages associated with each of the time management tools. One member from each team will share them with the class.

Time management tools	Advantages

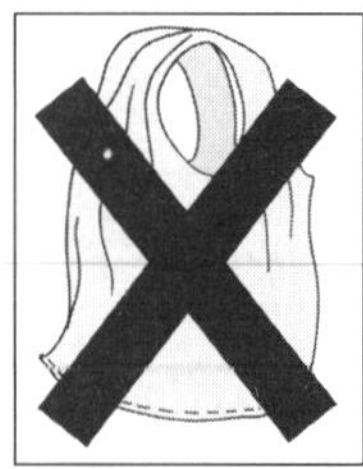

Speaking Exercise 3

You went to a shop to purchase groceries. You see the shopkeeper packing all the groceries in plastic bags, which are hazardous. Now that you know how dangerous these plastic bags are, try to educate the shopkeeper and also tell about the alternatives. Enact this situation.

Writing

Report Writing

What Is a Report?

A report can be defined as a communication in which the writer gives information to some individual or organization because it is his or her responsibility to do so. It is an assigned communication for a specific purpose and for a specific recipient. The common element in all reports is the element of responsibility. The writer is obliged to communicate a particular piece of information to those who need it as a part of his or her assigned, clearly defined and time-bound task.

The Purpose of a Report

A report is primarily a source of information to the management or an individual to help in decision making. It can also be used to offer a solution to a business problem. Its purpose can be

- to give information about a company's activities, progress, plans and problems;
- to record events for future reference in decision making;
- to recommend specific action;
- to justify and persuade readers about the need for action in controversial situations;
- to present facts to the management to help decide the direction the business should choose.

The basic purpose of a report is to help the management identify the reasons underlying a situation that the management is aware of.

Guidelines for Defining Report Objectives

Consider the objectives of a report from the point of view of its recipients and ask the following questions:

- For whom is the report written?
- What is their level of information and education?
- How much do they already know about the problem?
- Why do these people want the report?
- What do they want to know, and in what detail?
- How does the report's conclusion help them? What do they want to understand, what action do they want to take, or what decision do they wish to come to?

Writing Reports

A report presents facts, conclusions, and recommendations in simple and clear words, in a logical and well-defined structure. The elements or parts of a full report, in the order of their sequence, are:

1. Cover
2. Title Page
3. Acknowledgement
4. Table of Contents
5. Executive Summary
6. Introduction
7. Discussion/Description
8. Conclusions
9. Recommendations
10. Appendix
11. List of References
12. Bibliography
13. Glossary
14. Index

The first five elements constitute the front matter, the next four elements form the main body, and the last five constitute the back matter.

Sample of a Short Formal Report

Report on the fall in profits at Shoppers Stop, Retail Store, Ansal Plaza, New Delhi 30 August 2002.

Terms of Reference

At the request of the General Manager, Shoppers Stop, in his letter of 16 July 2002 (ref PO/LT/44/03), the author was instructed to

1. investigate the reasons for the fall in profits at the Shoppers Stop, Ansal Plaza, during the period 1 January 2002 to 30 June 2002;
2. make recommendations in the light of the findings.

Procedure

1. The sales records for the period 1 January–30 June 2002 were inspected and compared with those for the second half of 2001.
2. Two hundred customers were interviewed over seven days (2–8 August).
3. The premises were carefully inspected, both internally and externally.
4. The store manager, three sales assistants and two cashiers were interviewed.
5. Recent developments in Khelgaon Marg and the surrounding area were noted.

Findings

1. Extent of the fall in profits.

   Profits fell from a monthly average of 8 per cent in the second half of 2002 to an average of 6 per cent in the first six months of 2002.
2. Factors contributing to the fall in profits.

Internal

- Since December 2001, the manager, Mr R. S. Shah, has had a number of domestic problems, which have clearly affected his efficiency, particularly in the training and supervision of staff.
- One of the cashiers, Ms P. Kurien, has been consistently discourteous to customers. A majority of the customers interviewed complained of her brusqueness and her negative attitude. She certainly made an unfavourable impression when interviewed. Ms Kurien had no satisfactory explanation to offer for her behaviour.
- The three sales assistants appointed between December and April to replace those who left for other jobs are inexperienced and inefficient. The RSM found that shelves had not been properly stocked and that the old stock had been kept on display after the 'sellby' date.

External

1. The opening in January 2002 of a new branch of Ebony, South Extension, half a mile from the Shoppers branch, has probably attracted customers chiefly by means of special offers and intensive advertising in the local press.
2. The completion of the flyover in March 2002 has diverted some trade from Khelgaon as a whole, as the new shopping mall at South Extension is now easily accessible.

Conclusions

1. The decline in profits is partly the result of external developments—most notably, increased competition and restricted access to the store.
2. The fall in performance of the manager, together with the inexperience or discourtesy of some of the staff, is an additional important factor.

Recommendations

It is recommended that

1. an advertising campaign be mounted in the local press, including details of a competition and special offers;
2. the manager be advised to raise the standard of his work;
3. Ms Kurien be issued with a verbal warning about her behaviour;
4. a training programme for the three sales assistants to be implemented immediately;
5. staff performance to be reviewed in six weeks time; and
6. the viability of the store to be reviewed in December 2002.

P. Misra

Sales Manager

Elements of a Long Formal Report

The Title Page

On the title page, mention the name and status of the author, the name of the department and the date of issue.

The title of the report should be short, clear and unambiguous.

Example:

A Feasibility Report on the Incorporation of Outdoor Health Education Activities in the ESCORTS Management Development Programme.

Acknowledgements

You should thank everyone associated with the assignment and preparation of your report. Be generous in expressing gratitude.

Cover Letter

A cover letter is usually written by the top management or the project guide as a preface or foreword to a report, reflecting the management's policy and interpretation of the report's findings, conclusions and recommendations. It forwards the report and specifies why it is being sent to that person. It is placed between the cover and the title page. It is never bound inside the report. It can be written as a memo, letter, or forwarding certificate.

Letter of Transmittal

A formal report is often accompanied by a letter to outside readers. Although the letter of transmittal is usually placed after the title page, it functions as a greeting to the reader.

The letter covers a summary of the findings, conclusions and recommendations to give an idea of the report. It is best written in a direct, conversational manner.

Contents

Long reports must have a table of contents placed after the acknowledgements and before the summary. It is an important element in a long formal report. The table of contents indicates the hierarchy of topics and their sequence.

Mention the main sections of your report in the contents exactly as they are worded in the text.

Example:

CONTENTS

Abstract and Executive Summary

An abstract or summary is placed immediately after the list of tables, or after the title page or on the title page itself. Normally, a report uses either an abstract or an executive summary, according to the length of the report or the expectations of the readers. The company practice may be to have both an abstract and executive summary with long reports.

A summary should

- give the context of report;
- provide most important findings, conclusions and recommendations; and
- act as a time saver for the busy management.

Example of an Abstract

A nonlinear finite element procedure for the pre- and postbuckling analysis of thin-walled box-section beam-columns is presented. The influence of local plate buckling upon the overall ultimate buckling behavior of the member is incorporated in the analysis by adopting a set of modified-stress versus strain curves for axially loaded plates. Factors such as residual stresses, associated with hot-rolled and cold-formed sections, and initial geometrical imperfections are accounted for in the analysis. A number of examples are presented to demonstrate the accuracy and efficiency of the method.

The first line provides brief information about the aim of the report.

The second line discusses the topics covered and the methodology used.

The third line states the results achieved.

Poor Technical Writing

The 15ATS series toggle switches, in excess of 200 in total, were subject to the extreme of temperatures caused by being in close proximity to the furnace. This in turn caused heat failure as the expansion of metal caused a fault whereby the metal connection fused. The heat of the furnace has to be over 600 degrees Fahrenheit before this effect takes place.

Concise and Easy to Read

Over 200 automatic toggle switches fused when the keypad melted as the furnace temperature rose to over 600 degrees Fahrenheit.

Writing Exercise 1

1. Write a report to the principal of your college on the necessity of maintaining green cover in the college campus.
2. Write a report to the Election Commissioner, Andhra Pradesh, about alleged incidents of rigging in the recently concluded elections.
3. Submit a detailed report to the principal of your college on college fest that was held recently.

Writing Exercise 2

1. Write a letter to the principal of your college for permitting you to go on a 10-day excursion to Kerala.
2. Write a letter to the Chief Electrical Engineer, APTRANSCO, to complain about the low voltage in your area.
3. Write a letter of complaint to the Manager, Hind Electronics, on the faulty functioning of a recently purchased refrigerator.

Pronunciation

Contractions

In spoken English, a shortened form of a word or combination of words is often used instead of the full form. For instance, 'can't' is a contraction of 'cannot'. You should learn to use contractions to speak English more naturally and fluently.

Listening Exercise 2

Listen to and repeat the following full forms and their contracted forms clearly.

I am	I'm	they would/they had	they'd
I have	I've	we are	we're
I will	I'll	we have	we've
I would/I had	I'd	we would/we had	we'd
it is/it has	it's	you are	you're
it will	it'll	you have	you've
it had	it'd	you will	you'll
he is/he has	he's	you would/you had	you'd
he will	he'll	are not	aren't
he would/he had	he'd	cannot	can't
she is/she has	she's	could not	couldn't
she will	she'll	dare not	daren't
she would/she had	she'd	did not	didn't
they are	they're	do not	don't
they have	they've	does not	doesn't
they will	they'll	had not	hadn't

has not	hasn't	shall not	shan't
have not	haven't	should not	shouldn't
is not	isn't	was not	wasn't
must not	mustn't	will not	won't
need not	needn't	would not	wouldn't
ought not	oughtn't		

Listening Exercise 3

Listen to and repeat the sentences below. Say the parts of the words in bold clearly.

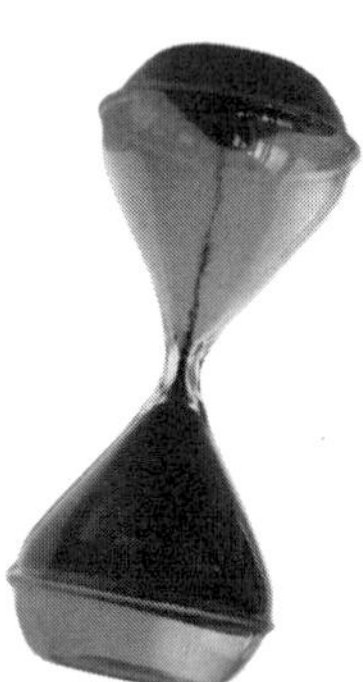

1. **I'd** like to work in a focused and effective way to accomplish my high-pay-off tasks.
2. Dinesh **doesn't** fritter his time away on conflicting priorities.
3. **She's** worked on strategically important tasks.
4. **We've** leant techniques to minimize the interruptions.
5. **He'd** rewarded himself for completing high-priority tasks in time.
6. **They've** devised ways to beat procrastination.
7. **He's** good at scheduling his time effectively.
8. I **don't** normally over-commit to others.
9. **I've** realized that careless decisions could kill time.

Write sentences beginning with the following:

1. I'm ______________________.
2. I've ______________________.
3. I'll ______________________.
4. I'd ______________________.
5. It's______________________.
6. It'll ______________________.
7. It'd ______________________.
8. He's ______________________.
9. He'll ______________________.
10. He'd ______________________.
11. She's ______________________.
12. She'll ______________________.
13. She'd ______________________.
14. They're ______________________.
15. They've ______________________.
16. They'll ______________________.
17. They ______________________.
18. We're ______________________.

19. We've ____________________.
20. We'd ____________________.
21. You're ____________________.
22. You've ____________________.
23. You'll ____________________.
24. You'd ____________________.
25. You aren't ____________________.
26. I can't ____________________.
27. She couldn't ____________________.
28. You daren't ____________________.
29. He didn't ____________________.
30. We don't ____________________.
31. It doesn't ____________________.
32. They hadn't ____________________.
33. She hasn't ____________________.
34. I haven't ____________________.
35. He isn't ____________________.
36. We mustn't ____________________.
37. You needn't ____________________.
38. I shan't ____________________.
39. We shouldn't ____________________.
40. It wasn't ____________________.

Vocabulary

Crossword Puzzle

The exercise given below is a crossword puzzle. The meanings of the words to be placed in the crossword are given under 'across' and 'down'. Think of a word for each meaning and place it in its respective place in the grid as instructed. The number within brackets indicates the number of letters you get for the word. Refer to the passage if you can't think of the correct word. One example is given for you.

h	a	n	g	i	n	g	
	4		5				
2				2			
						5	6
		3					
3							
4							

Across

1. The act of killing someone by tying a rope around their neck and suspending them. (7)

   answer: hanging
2. An ugly sight in a public place. (7)
3. To block something or become blocked. (8)
4. To damage something badly. (7)
5. To throw something in an untidy way. (4)

Down

1. Clean and likely to prevent infections or disease from spreading. (7)
2. Gas that is necessary for human beings to live. (6)
3. Harmful or poisonous, especially used for gases. (7)
4. An object for the children to play with. (4)
5. Something that is dangerous. (6)
6. Anything that is grown without using chemicals (7)

Functional Grammar

Articles

A, **an** and **the** are called articles. 'A' and 'an' are referred to as indefinite articles. 'The' is called the definite article.
A and **an** are used:

1. When talking about nouns in a general way or when newly introduced

   Examples:

   I have just heard a **bird** sing.

   An **airplane** took off a few minutes ago.

Note that 'a' is used before words beginning with a consonant sound and 'an' is used before words beginning with a vowel sound. This should not be confused with whether the letter of the alphabet that the word begins with is a vowel or a consonant.

Examples:

a boy,	an engineer,	a girl,
an elephant,	a teacher,	an animal,
a driver,	an article,	an hour,
a one rupee note,	an honest person,	a one-eyed person

2. Before nouns that are meant to be examples of a class of things

   Examples:

   A **cow** gives milk.

   A **computer** can multi-task.

3. With expressions of price, speed, etc.

   Examples:

   He rode the bike at fifty kilometres an **hour**.

   Rice costs twenty rupees a **kilogram**.

4. Before a proper noun when referring to specific qualities

   Examples:

   Only a **Sehwag** can hit such shots.

   Only a **Newton** can answer this question.

5. To indicate membership in a profession, nation, or religion

   Examples:

   Vinod is a **painter**.

   Jane is an **Irishman**.

   Tharuni is a practising **Buddhist**.

The is used:

1. With nouns that have already been mentioned and are referred to again

   Example:

   A **man** went for a walk with his dog. The **man** fell into a well and the dog began to bark. A passer-by pulled the man out of the well.

2. With a singular countable noun that stands for a whole class

   Examples:

   The **bicycle** is the **common man's** vehicle.

   The **lion** is a fierce wild animal.

3. Before a noun which is the only one of its kind in a given situation

   Examples:

   The **teacher** wrote an outline of a story on the **black-board**.

   The **principal** is not in town.

4. Before a noun that is specified or made definite by the addition of a qualifying word, phrase or clause

   Examples:

   The **tall man** is the **head** of this institute.

   The **beggar** in the corner is a policeman in disguise.

5. Before an adjective to turn it into a noun with a plural meaning

   Example:

   The rich are getting richer and **the poor** are getting poorer.

   The rich = rich people

   The poor = poor people

6. Before the names of mountains, rivers, oceans, seas, groups of islands, etc.

   Examples:

   the Himalayas, the Red Sea, the Ganga, the Laccadives, the Indian Ocean

7. To refer to a whole family

   Examples:

   the Nehrus, the Gandhis, the Kennedys

8. Before adjectives in the superlative degree when we make comparisons

   Example:

   He owns the most expensive car in the city.

Omission of Articles

The is not used:

1. With **uncountable nouns** referring to something in a general sense

   Examples:

   Tea is a popular drink.

   Beauty lies in the eyes of the beholder.

2. Before names of continents, countries, cities and towns

   Examples:

   Asia, Africa, India, China, Tokyo, Wall Street

3. Before names of sports

   Examples:

   cricket, football, tennis

4. Before names of academic subjects

   Examples:

   physics, chemistry, maths, history

5. Before abstract nouns

   Examples:

   Modesty is a virtue.

   Anger can make you go out of control.

6. Before mass nouns

   Examples:

   Gold is a precious metal.

   Air and **water** are indispensable to man.

7. Before nouns such as school, church, bed, hospital, when their primary purpose (study, attending service, treatment for illness, etc.) is referred to

   Example:

   He goes to **school** at 10 a.m. every day.

8. Before 'man' and 'woman' when used in a general sense

   Example:

   Man is a social animal.

9. After expressions such as 'sort of', 'type of', 'kind of', 'manner of'

   Example:

   What **sort of** person are you?

10. With phrases like 'by bus', 'by plane', 'by messenger', 'by car', 'by sea', 'by post', 'on foot', 'by train', etc.

    Example:

    They travelled by **sea**.

Fill in the blanks with 'a', 'an' or 'the' where necessary:

1. Could you please tell me how to get to ____________ railway station?
2. Yes, take the second turn on the right, walk past ____________ parade grounds and take the first turn on ____________ left.
3. I forgot ____________ book in ____________ library. Could you get it for me?
4. ____________ fire broke out in ____________ busy shopping mall. ____________ fire-brigade could not bring it under control even after struggling for many hours as they did not have ____________ right equipment.
5. ____________ flight crashed into ____________ Atlantic ocean a few days ago. All ____________ passengers on board died.

Place 'a', 'an' or 'the' wherever necessary and rewrite each of the following sentences:

1. Delhi is capital of India.
2. We travelled by train to most beautiful part of the place of that country.
3. I went to return book I borrowed from library, but librarians were not there.
4. She read Ramayana, Quran and Bible when she was small kid.
5. He wrote extraordinary novel.

Fill in the blanks below using articles where necessary:

1. a) Is there ____________ park nearby?

   b) Let's take a walk in ____________ park for a while.
2. a) They had dinner in ____________ very nice restaurant.

   b) This restaurant is ____________ most expensive one in ____________ town.
3. a) Has ____________ newborn baby been given a name yet?

   b) What's ____________ name of person we met this morning?
4. a) There isn't ____________ airport near where I live. ____________ nearest airport is several miles away.

   b) Our flight was delayed. We had to wait at ____________ airport for three hours.
5. a) "Are you going away next week?" No, ____________ week after next.'

   b) I'm going away for ____________ week in September.

Prepositions

A preposition is a word that shows the relation between words in a sentence.

In the sentences 'He jumped off the wall', and 'She walked on the beach', 'off' and 'on' are prepositions.

A List of Prepositions

in	to	during
at	into	while
over	at	beside
among	by	since
on	next to	besides
by	instead of	in addition to
off	for	apart from

Uses of Prepositions

Below are some commonly used prepositions along with their usage:

For is used to refer to a period of time.

Example:

I have been waiting for two hours.

During is used to refer to something that happens over a particular period of time.

Example:

I met a lot of people during my last holiday.

By is used to mean 'not later than'.

Example:

You must be here by 6 o'clock.

Until and **till** are used to refer to how long a situation continues.

Example:

We can't start the programme till the chief guest arrives.

At is used in expressions like:

at the moment, at the same time, at night, at the weekend, at Christmas

at the party, at her house, at the company, at the station, at the airport, at the post office, at the age of five, at a great speed, at 90 degree Celsius

In is used in expressions like:

in the morning, in the afternoon, in the evening, in a minute, in the next few days, in a couple of weeks

in Hyderabad, in a village, in a small town,

in bed, in hospital, in prison, in a line, in a picture, in the world

in the shade/sun/rain

On is used in expressions like:

on Sunday, on Saturday, on 12 March, on the first day of the week

on the left, on the right, on the way

on a bus, on an island, on horseback

on a holiday/trip/cruise

on TV/ the radio/strike/purpose

Verbs with Prepositions

accuse of	amazed at	annoyed with
angry with/over	apologize to	apply to
aware of	care for	congratulate on
consist of	decide on/about	delighted with
depend on	die of	dream about/of
furious about	good at	leave for
live on	look for/after/at	search for
shout at	similar to	smile at
sorry for/about	suffer from	talk to
think about/of	tired of	write to

Fill in the blanks with appropriate prepositions:

1. I congratulated him ____________ his success.
2. We were amazed ____________ her dance performance.
3. No one approves ____________ copying in the exams.
4. I'm looking forward ____________ meeting my old friends.
5. She left ____________ France last week.
6. We works a lot ____________ the afternoons.
7. They rested for a while ____________ the shade.
8. The workers went ____________ a strike.
9. She is not doing anything ____________ the moment.
10. They are searching ____________ some articles.

Spelling

Look at the sets of words below and circle the word with the correct spelling. Check your answers with the other members of your team. If you need to, use a good dictionary to find the correct spelling.

1.	cantingency	contingensy	contengency	contingency
2.	manegement	management	managment	managemant
3.	priority	priorrity	proirity	priorety
4.	procrastinete	proccrastinate	procrastanate	procrastinate
5.	purposefull	purpuseful	purposeful	parposeful
6.	succesful	successfull	successful	sucessful
7.	proverb	provarb	provverb	prroverb
8.	evidance	eviddence	evidence	evidenc
9.	megazine	magazzine	magazine	magazin
10.	interuption	interruption	intterruption	intteruption

APPENDIXES

Appendix 1

Regular Verbs

A regular verb is a verb that forms its past tense and past participle by adding '-d' or '-ed'.

Present tense form	Past tense and past participle form
accept	accepted
advise	advised
approve	approved
bat	batted
bless	blessed
blink	blinked
call	called
continue	continued
copy	copied
chew	chewed
decay	decayed
disappear	disappeared
drop	dropped
earn	earned
embarrass	embarrassed
expand	expanded
face	faced
fetch	fetched
float	floated
guarantee	guaranteed
guess	guessed
guide	guided
hand	handed
hang	hanged
harass	harassed
imagine	imagined
influence	influenced
interfere	interfered
invite	invited
joke	joked
judge	judged
juggle	juggled

Present tense form	Past tense and past participle form
kiss	kissed
kneel	kneeled
laugh	laughed
lie	lied
load	loaded
memorize	memorized
mix	mixed
move	moved
name	named
net	netted
notice	noticed
object	objected
order	ordered
own	owned
pause	paused
persuade	persuaded
pour	poured
question	questioned
queue	queued
refuse	refused
rescue	rescued
rock	rocked
scribble	scribbled
shelter	sheltered
squeeze	squeezed
surround	surrounded
talk	talked
thank	thanked
type	typed
undress	undressed
unite	united

(Continued)

(Continued)

Present tense form	Past tense and past participle form
use	used
vanish	vanished
veer	veered
veto	vetoed
waddle	waddled
wobble	wobbled

Present tense form	Past tense and past participle form
wonder	wondered
wrap	wrapped
yawn	yawned
yell	yelled
zip	zipped
zoom	zoomed

Appendix 2

Irregular Verbs

An irregular verb is a verb that does not form its past tense and past participle by adding '-d' or '-ed'.

Present tense form	Past tense form	Past participle form
be	was, were	been
beat	beat	beaten
cost	cost	cost
cut	cut	cut
deal	dealt	dealt
eat	ate	eaten
fall	fell	fallen
feel	felt	felt
find	found	found
fly	flew	flown
lie	lay	lain
mean	meant	meant
read	read	read
rise	rose	risen
shine	shone	shone

Appendix 3

Tenses Chart with Active and Passive Verb Forms

Study the following table that gives the active and passive verb forms of the twelve tenses in English:

Tense	Simple	Continuous	Perfect	Perfect continuous	
ACTIVE	He drafts a report.	He is drafting a report.	He has drafted a report.	He has been drafting a report.	PRESENT
PASSIVE	A report is drafted by him.	A report is being drafted by him.	A report has been drafted by him.	No passive form	
ACTIVE	He drafted a report.	He was drafting a report.	He had drafted a report.	He had been drafting a report.	PAST
PASSIVE	A report was drafted by him.	A report was being drafted by him.	A report had been drafted by him.	No passive form	
ACTIVE	He will draft a report.	He will be drafting a report.	He will have drafted a report.	He will have been drafting a report.	FUTURE
PASSIVE	A report will be drafted by him.	No passive form	A report will have been drafted by him.	No passive form	

Appendix 4

Errors Often Made by Indian Students

Incorrect	Correct
Will I leave now?	May I leave now?
This hall shall not accommodate 20 people.	This hall will not accommodate 20 people.
I shall hope that you will complete your project by next week.	I shall hope that you will complete your project by next week.
My teacher insists that I could submit the assignment by tomorrow.	My teacher insists that I should submit the assignment by tomorrow.
Our culture suggests that we might respect our elders.	Our culture suggests that we should respect our elders.
Do you think I may accept this offer?	Do you think I should accept this offer?
Might you have a bright future.	May you have a bright future.
Will I please use your telephone?	Could I please use your telephone?
We could overcome our problems if we need to complete the task in time.	We should overcome our problems if we need to complete the task in time.
I may not do this as my parents will be very angry when they come to know about this.	I must not do this as my parents will be very angry when they come to know about this.
We doesn't understand his behaviour.	We don't understand his behaviour.
He haven't secured good marks.	He hasn't secured good marks.
None of them take his advice seriously.	None of them takes his advice seriously.
Many accidents has been reported on this road.	Many accidents have been reported on this road.
I will call you back after I will reach home.	I will call you back after I reach home.
We have been knowing each other for five years.	We have known each other for five years.

(Continued)

(Continued)

Incorrect	Correct
He was carved a niche for himself.	He carved a niche for himself.
Neither Kiran nor his parents is going to come to the party.	Neither Kiran nor his parents are going to come to the party.
The teacher, as well as her students, are excited about the educational tour.	The teacher, as well as her students, is excited about the educational tour.
These scissors is very sharp.	These scissors are very sharp.
He did not do well in the GD because which he was not selected for personal interview round.	He did not do well in the GD, because of which he was not selected for personal interview round.
Prakash is normally very unruffled, although he's being very agitated today.	Prakash is normally very unruffled, whereas he's being very agitated today.
Saritha hasn't reached home still.	Saritha hasn't reached home yet.
He didn't speak persuasively consequently didn't leave much impact on the audience.	He didn't speak persuasively for which didn't leave much impact on the audience.
You could submit your work now, or otherwise, you incorporate the changes suggested and submit it after a week.	You could submit your work now, or alternatively, you incorporate the changes suggested and submit it after a week.
Shashidhar is by and large the best business person in the town.	Shashidhar is by far the best business person in the town.
He went on lecturing as the audience were restless.	He went on lecturing although the audience were restless.
Ramya has been ecstatic ever after she won the trophy.	Ramya has been ecstatic ever since she won the trophy.
Despite of heavy rain students attended the class.	Despite heavy rain students attended the class.
For traffic chaos, commuting has become a nightmare.	Because of traffic chaos, commuting has become a nightmare.
It is an unique event.	It is a unique event.
The rich should help poor.	The rich should help the poor.
I don't understand what a sort of person is she?	I don't understand what sort of person is she?
I sent the book by the post.	I sent the book by post.
He sat on the corner.	He sat in the corner.
How come you are not seen on this photograph?	How come you are not seen in this photograph?
They quarreled for silly things.	They quarrelled over silly things.
I am working in an university.	I am working in a university.
My father is a MLA.	My father is an MLA.
I will reach home in a hour	I will reach home in an hour.
Lots of trees have cut down.	Lots of trees have been cut down.
The police were arrested the thief.	The police arrested the thief.
We asked to get our projects ready by next Saturday.	We were asked to get our projects ready by next Saturday.
The government must be done something about ragging.	The government must do something about ragging.
My friend was given this suggestion to me.	My friend gave this suggestion to me.
She has been doing many tasks at the same time, hasn't been she?	She has been doing many tasks at the same time, hasn't she?

He should know how to draft a report, should he?	He should know how to draft a report, shouldn't he?
He has given a great speech, has he?	He has given a great speech, hasn't he?
You won't buckle under pressure, do you?	You won't buckle under pressure, will you?
You don't know where the post office is, will you?	You don't know where the post office is, do you?
He told to me that he had understood the lesson.	He told me that he had understood the lesson.
She told that she would be there tomorrow.	She said that she would be there tomorrow.
He asked me what was multi-tasking.	He asked me what multi-tasking was.
He said, "Wow, we managed to complete our project in time".	He said, "Wow, we managed to complete our project in time".
"I am doing a workshop on email etiquette", said he.	"I am doing a workshop on email etiquette", he said.
My mother asked me not to waste my time.	My mother advised me not to waste my time.
He said if these techniques were useful.	He asked if these techniques were useful.
If I were you I will not pursue this course.	If I were you I would not pursue this course.
If he had attended the classes regularly he would understand the concepts easily.	If he had attended the classes regularly he would have understood the concepts easily.
If you work in a planned manner, you were bound to sound in whatever you do.	If you work in a planned manner, you are bound to sound in whatever you do.

Appendix 5

Spelling Rules

1. Most words add 's' to the root forms without any change **(tree–trees)**.
2. Words ending in 's', 'sh', 'ch', 'ss', 'x', and 'z', usually add 'es' to form the plural **(bus–buses)**.
3. Words ending in a consonant and 'y', change the 'y' to 'i' and add 'es' **(party– parties)**.
4. Some words ending in 'f' change the 'f' to 'v' and add 'es' **(calf–calves)**.
5. Some singular words have different words for their plural form **(man–men; mouse–mice; goose–geese)**.
6. Many words are formed by adding 'ed' and 'ing' without any change **(play–played–playing)**.
7. Words ending in a silent 'e' drop the 'e' before adding 'ed' and 'ing' **(smile–smiled–smiling)**.
8. Words ending in a consonant and 'y' change the 'y' to 'i' before adding 'ed', but do not make any change when adding 'ing' **(rely–relied–relying)**.
9. Words ending in a vowel and 'y' add 'ed' and 'ing' without making any other change **(delay–delayed–delaying)**.
10. Words of one syllable ending in a single consonant preceded by a single vowel double the final consonant before adding 'ed' and 'ing' **(trim–trimmed–trimming)**.
11. Words of two or more syllables double the final consonant before adding 'ed' and 'ing' when these conditions are met: the last syllable ends in a single consonant preceded by a single vowel, and the accent is on the last syllable **(refer–referred–referring)**.

TRANSCRIPTS

Unit 1

Listening Exercise 1

Personality comes from the Greek word 'persona', meaning 'mask'. In a general sense, personality refers to the combination of behaviours that a person possesses. Your personality is commonly thought of as something that distinguishes you from others.

You must also understand that developing an impressive personality is something that can't happen overnight. It's a conscious and focused effort, rather than simply a matter of luck.

There are many factors that influence your personality: these are genetic, environmental, and social in nature. Take some time to look at how these factors are shaping your personality. How do your education level, your caste and class background, the neighbourhood you live in, etc., affect the way you see and understand life? Alternatively, you can also use these factors to study the personality of others.

Try the following to mould yourself into a well-rounded personality:

- **Have a vision:** Having a concrete vision of a future that is in line with your values, interests and desires helps you to make it real.
- **Imagine yourself becoming what you want to be:** You must form a mental picture of who you are and who you want to be. This will help you to focus on your goals.
- **Be clear about your goals:** Your goals, both short- and long-term, must be clear, and you should devise proper plans to achieve them. Lack of goal-orientation is the reason many people don't succeed in life.
- **Be assertive:** Assertiveness means communicating what you want in a clear manner, and expressing your feelings, opinions, and needs firmly.
- **Be mentally sound:** If you are mentally sound, you will realize your own abilities. You can cope with the stress of life, and work productively and fruitfully.
- **Be physically fit:** The maxim "a sound mind in a sound body" means that if you don't take care of your body, you can't have a sound mind. Exercise on a regular basis and eat nutritious food so that you can function better and enjoy life fully.
- **Be spiritually strong:** A spiritual person knows that we are all one, and consciously attempts to honour this oneness. A spiritual person is a kind person. If you're are not spiritually strong, you'll find it difficult to make sense of the world, and will lapse into negative actions or thoughts.
- **Build your confidence:** If you are confident in yourself you will be able to achieve your goals untiringly. As much as success builds confidence, confidence also builds success. They feed off each other.
- **Communicate effectively:** Your ability to communicate your feelings, emotions and ideas effectively is crucial to your success. Effective communication will strengthen your existing relationships and help you to form positive bonds in future interactions.
- **Cultivate a sense of humour:** Cultivating a sense of humour not only makes life more bearable, it makes you more attractive to others. Try to see the funny side of situations and think of stories and items that would make people laugh. Laughing at others is not funny, but laughing at your own mistakes and behaviours is. It also makes you more approachable.
- **Deal with people on a win-win basis:** In life you should only get what you deserve. You must expect things to work for the mutual advantage of people concerned in every situation. If you expect to gain at the cost of other people, you become greedier. Don't ever think, "I win, you lose".
- **Develop a sense of appreciation:** You will find the world to be a beautiful place if you cultivate a sense of appreciation. Look for opportunities to express your appreciation as frequently as possible, as this is bound to affect your mental and spiritual well-being. This attitude will help you to count your blessings.
- **Develop critical thinking:** Critical thinking has nothing to do with criticism; rather, it is logical and purposeful judgement about what to do or what to believe. Critical thinking is very important for you to stay balanced. You won't be easily deceived or cheated if you have a critical mind.
- **Develop your creativity:** When you are creative, you are trying to be original, imaginative and valuable. These are essential to your success in every field.
- **Have a sense of gratitude:** You need to be thankful for everything that you have. The more you express your gratitude to the people who deserve it, the nobler you become.

- **Have self-esteem:** You must hold yourself in high regard so that you can channel your energies to achieve success. If you don't have a sense of self-worth, your life will be miserable.
- **Be self-motivated:** You must motivate yourself to find the strength to do things you want to do without relying on others. Self-motivation can keep your spirits high even when the situation is discouraging. Have bigger goals and cultivate a 'never give up' attitude to help you motivate yourself.
- **Learn the ways to overcome failure:** The proverb "failures are the stepping stones to success" helps you to view failures in a right perspective. A failure gives you an opportunity to learn more and more about things you do.
- **Learn to deal with criticism:** Respond to criticism with nobility, detachment or objectivity. When criticism is constructive, value it and learn from it. Learn to brush aside criticism that comes from spite or jealousy. Don't take it too personally.
- **Learn to empathize:** You must try to understand people's emotions and feelings by putting yourself in their shoes. This ability helps you to be sensitive rather than cold-hearted.
- **Manage your stress and anger well:** While anger is often productive, it often adds to stress. Rather than trying to suppress the anger, you should try to cut the anger triggers from your life. Ask yourself what makes you angry and see if you can remove the causes of the anger. Added stress can make you more anger-prone. Therefore, having stress management techniques on hand can help you remove anger from your life. Some techniques that are especially useful are breathing exercises: A few deep breaths can calm your stress response and enable you to feel more in control in virtually any situation.
- **Mature with age:** This means that you have to look at things from a broader perspective as you age.
- **Never be complacent:** To be complacent is to be pleased with oneself and one's situation. While confidence and happiness are really good for yourself, complacency leads to boredom and stops you from growing as a person. Strike a balance between being complacent and over-ambitious.
- **Think positively:** The world is how you look at it. Nourish yourself on good things, and discard the bad.
- **Value relationships:** Your life becomes much more pleasurable when you value your relationship with family, friends and others. Be generous with what you can give to others but do not expect too much of others.
- **Be a role model:** Feel proud about your achievements. Share your stories of success and failure with others so that they can learn from them. Live your life trying to contribute as much as you can to your family and the society.

We're sure you'll become great personalities by consciously following the points we've shared with you. Thank you for your time, and we wish you success in all your endeavours.

Listening Exercise 2

Listen to these words and repeat after the speaker. Note how certain parts of the words are stressed.

1. a**ffec**tionate
2. a**nnoy**ing
3. **boi**sterous
4. **cu**nning
5. **domineer**ing
6. dy**na**mic
7. **di**ffident
8. enig**ma**tic
9. **em**pa**the**tic
10. **gu**llible
11. mag**na**nimous
12. ma**ni**pulative
13. opti**mis**tic
14. pessi**mis**tic
15. **vi**sionary

Listening Exercise 3

Listen to these words and note how the pronunciation changes with the part of speech.

rebel (noun) The rebels overthrew the dictator.

re**bel** (verb) Rakesh rebelled against the system when he was very young.

convert (noun) Smitha is a religious **con**vert.

con**vert** (verb) She con**ver**ted herself recently.

Unit 2

Listening Exercise 1

Speaker 1: Hi, I'm Manisha. I'm here to express my views on capital punishment. I strongly feel that the death penalty is necessary. I believe that capital punishment acts as a deterrent. My intuition tells me that it will deter criminals from killing. Ridding ourselves of capital punishment on account of its brutality would be neither decent nor rational. Until people find a better way to prevent crime, the death penalty is our strongest defence.

Several religious scriptures too require the death penalty for a wide variety of crimes. I support the death penalty as many people feel that killing convicted murderers will satisfy their need for justice and/or vengeance. They feel that certain crimes are so heinous that executing the criminal is the only reasonable response.

The death penalty is also warranted in view of public safety. Once a convicted murderer is executed, there is no chance that he will break out of jail and cause harm again. I also believe that the death penalty serves to respect the value of human life. Edward Koch echoed the same when he said, "It is by exacting the highest penalty for the taking of human life that we affirm the highest value of human life."

I'd like to conclude by saying that the working benefits of capital punishment outweigh its demerits.

Speaker 2: Hello everyone, I'm Sushma. I'm here to express my views on capital punishment. We sometimes hear of governments putting people, who later turned out to be innocent, on death row. If we are not entirely sure that a convicted murderer is really guilty, does the government have the right to decide if they are to die? Many murderers who are imprisoned for life are later found innocent, and have been pardoned. It is impossible to pardon a corpse.

The death penalty has not been proven effective in reducing homicide rates. As we all know, people murder for a variety of reasons and in many different situations, often when they are not in a rational frame of mind. It may be hopeless to expect any form of punishment to act as a deterrent when the murderer isn't thinking straight while committing the crime.

I also believe that we need to forgive and forget. We have to remember that we are only human, and we do make mistakes. Yes, I do agree that if someone has committed a serious crime, then that person should be punished. But I don't think people deserve to be killed for it. We have no right to take someone's life away from them even though they have committed a terrible crime. I'm also of the view that the idea of the death penalty negates our belief in the human capacity for change. Moreover, it reinforces the idea that killing is a proper way of responding to those who have wronged us.

There are many other things that could be done to punish the guilty. Why choose the wrong one?

Listening Exercise 2

The term 'euthanasia' comes from the Greek word for 'easy death'. Also referred to as 'mercy killing', euthanasia is the act of killing or helping someone commit suicide to prevent suffering. Basically, euthanasia is killing in the name of compassion. We sometimes hear of people who suffer from terminal illnesses or an incurable condition going to court for the right to end their life. Some of you know that in many countries, including our own, mercy killings are against the law. Let us discuss this topic and see what points emerge for and against euthanasia.

Archana: I think that mercy killing should be allowed. However, precautions should be taken to prevent its misuse. A medical board under the control of the government should be constituted to monitor the cases involving terminally ill patients.

Swati: I'm completely against it. It has nothing to do with mercy at all. No one, including the best doctors, can tell for sure whether the patient can be saved or not.

Manoj: I think euthanasia should be legal. If a person is suffering from an incurable ailment and is unable to bear the pain, there is no reason to force them to suffer.

Swati: I recently read a report about the practice of euthanasia in the Netherlands. The gist of it is that legalization of physician-assisted suicide might weaken society's resolve to expand services and resources aimed at caring for dying patients.

Manoj: I agree with that. I also read a survey according to which a majority of respondents felt that it may be misused in India.

Swati: But if we don't allow mercy killing how can we relieve the patient from extreme pain?

Manoj: Shouldn't it also be viewed as a case of freedom of choice? This would also be important when medical expenses are too high for the family.

Swati: But what if the right becomes an obligation? Besides, when someone's pain is relieved that person usually wants to go on living. Medical professionals need to think of ways to kill pain without killing the patient.

Manoj: Does this mean we need a 'right to die' law? Also, supposing a dying person has the right to hasten his own death, does he require the help of doctors and nurses to do so? Should they be held culpable?

Archana: It's easy to imagine a doctor giving a lethal dose of a pain-killing drug and then claiming that death was the best way to eliminate physical suffering. If the doctor could also show that the patient had requested the lethal dosage, the court might well interpret the law in the doctor's favour.

Swati: Let me also tell you how legalized euthanasia could be misused. According to a report from the Netherlands, in 1990, over a thousand patients were killed without their consent. Of over 22,000 deaths due to withdrawal of life support, about 60 per cent were denied medical treatment without their consent. Twelve per cent of the patients who were mentally competent weren't even consulted.

Manoj: We need to think of the potential for abuse if mercy killing becomes legal. What if someone stands to inherit a huge amount when someone dies? Wouldn't an heir find it tempting to nudge that person in the direction of a lethal injection?

Swati: The alternatives are appropriate medical care—including the withdrawal of treatment upon the patient's request—or if that treatment serves no therapeutic purpose, dispensing the drugs necessary to control pain.

Manoj: I think we need to wrap up our discussion as we are running out of time. In conclusion, we might say that emphasis must be on care and comfort for the dying. Try to make their lives better, and this will reduce the attractiveness of legalized euthanasia. Thank you.

Listening Exercise 3

Listen to these sentences and repeat after the speaker. Note how stress on different words in the sentences changes the meaning.

She—argued—logically.

She argued logically.

She **argued** logically.

She argued **logically**.

They—noticed—many—logical—fallacies—in—his—speech.

They noticed many logical fallacies in his speech.

They **noticed** many logical fallacies in his speech.

They noticed **many** logical fallacies in his speech.

They noticed many **logical** fallacies in his speech.

They noticed many logical **fallacies** in his speech.

They noticed many logical fallacies in **his** speech.

They noticed many logical fallacies in his **speech**.

Unit 3

Listening Exercise 1

Hi. In this short talk I'm going to share a few tips about goal-orientation. At the outset I'd like to say that setting clear, written goals and implementing them with perseverance is necessary for success. In fact, your life becomes more purposeful, productive and fruitful if you have worthy goals. Academic, professional and personal success is possible only if you set your goals.

Now, I'm going to tell you more about how to set your goals. You can follow the W-A-S-T WAST rule to set your goals.

WAST stands for:

W – Worthy—your goals must be socially acceptable

A – Attainable—set realistic goals, taking into account ground realities and the resources available to you

S – Specific—your goals must be clear and precise

T – Time bound—set a reasonable time frame for achieving your goals

In addition to these, you should also bear in mind the following:

1. Write down your goals.
2. State each goal as a positive statement.
3. Be precise.
4. Do not set goals too low or too high.

To achieve your goals, keep three things in mind:

One, create to-do lists

Two, prioritize your goals

Three, follow the P-E-E-R PEER principle. PEER stands for:

P – Plan—create a list of tasks to be achieved

E – Execute—implement your plans

E – Evaluate—assess your progress, considering what went well and what went wrong

R – Reset—reset your goals based on your evaluation

Now, let me give you seven important areas for goal-setting. These are attitude, career, education, family, finance, fitness, and social service. Think of some short-term and long-term goals for these seven important areas in life.

I hope these points will help you to set goals and achieve them in style. Thanks, and all the best!

Listening Exercise 2

Hi, guys! I'm Geetha. I'm a first-year engineering student. Well, I wish to do very well in my studies. I'd like to take up challenging topics with practical utility for my project work. I wish to become a famous engineer in the next 10 years. I'd love to come up with several innovations that will usher in far-reaching changes in society. I'd like to be known as an innovative engineer with social commitment.

Hi! I'm Aravind. I wish to become a great motivational speaker within the next 10 years. I'd like to enlighten people on several issues. I wish to concentrate on helping people to make the best use of resources. I'll also impress upon them how these resources should be preserved for future generations. I'll also use all my knowledge to help people lead an eco-friendly life.

Hi, folks! I'm Priyanka. I hope to become an entrepreneur ten years down the line. I'd like to be known as person with exemplary corporate ethics. I wish to prove the point that profits can be made by following higher principles rather than resorting to deceptive methods. I won't be the person who makes the mistake of equating practicality with greed. Moreover, I wish to conduct my business with social responsibility. In fact, I'd love to live life abiding by the adage, "Honesty is the best policy".

Listening Exercise 3

Listen to these words and repeat after the speaker. Listen carefully for word stress:

1. **ex**ecute exe**cu**tion
2. e**va**luate evalu**a**tion
3. de**ter**mine de**ter**mi**na**tion
4. **im**plement implemen**ta**tion
5. con**tend** con**ten**tion
6. at**tend** at**ten**tion
7. sepa**rate** sepa**ra**tion
8. de**ci**de de**ci**sion
9. re**peat** repe**ti**tion
10. priori**tize** prioriti**za**tion

Listening Exercise 4

Listen to these sentences and repeat after the speaker. Note the way certain syllables are stressed.

1. She **wants** to a**chieve** her **goals quick**ly.
2. Re**mem**ber to **write** your **goals** pre**cise**ly.
3. They pur**sued** their **dreams** with a **great** de**ter**mi**na**tion.
4. The **start**ing point of **all** a**chieve**ment is de**sire**.
5. He be**came** a **pro**minent perso**na**lity in a **short time**.
6. We de**pend**ed on the **pro**ven **me**thods to at**tai**n our **as**pi**ra**tions.
7. They prog**ress**ed re**mar**kably **well**.
8. We trans**form**ed our **lives to**tally.
9. They **faced se**veral **trials** and tribu**la**tions.
10. He s**how**ed an in**dom**itable **spirit** and over**came** insur**moun**table **pro**blems.

Unit 4

Listening Exercise 1

Student: Ma'am, can you tell me something about teamwork?

Teacher: Well, simply put, teamwork is working with others in order to accomplish tasks.

Student: I've heard that employers often want their employees to work in teams.

Teacher: That's right. Every organization has its own goals, and only if the staff work together will they be able to achieve their goals efficiently. Organizations believe that teamwork at its best results in a synergy that can be very productive.

Student: What does 'synergy' mean, ma'am?

Teacher: Synergy can be defined as the combined power of a group of individuals when they are working together, which is greater than the total power achieved by each individual working separately.

Student: Can you tell me about the qualities that are required to work in teams effectively?

Teacher: To be able to work in teams effectively you must have good interpersonal skills, optimism, a co-operative and friendly nature, adaptability, and the ability to communicate effectively.

Student: Could you tell me a little more about them?

Teacher: Yes, let me try to explain each of them in detail. Interpersonal skills refer to your ability to get along with others. To be good at this you need to communicate appropriately with your team members, and listen to the ideas and concerns of each and every one.

Remember that others will want to work with you only if you exude confidence and optimism. You have to focus on the positive. This involves learning from your setbacks and being confident about achieving good results even in the face of several difficulties.

As a good team player, you need to cooperate and not compete with other members of your team. This helps the team stay united and achieve goals without much conflict.

Be adaptable. You must be open to other points of view. Learn to cultivate a give-and-take attitude. Others will resent you if you are too opposed to new concepts or change.

You need to be able to communicate your ideas clearly and freely. You must also have good persuasive skills so that you can convince your fellow team members to support your ideas.

Student: What else do I need to function efficiently in a team?

Teacher: Apart from these, you must also be able to understand the roles and tasks clearly. Be methodical and planned in your work. Be ready to handle the stress that accompanies deadlines and other limitations and constraints. Use time wisely so that you can stick to the schedule and meet your deadline.

Student: Thank you very much for your time.

Teacher: You're welcome! I'm glad you found this information useful. Good luck!

Listening Exercise 2

Listen to these words and repeat after the speaker:

1. beam ream seem team
2. fame game name shame
3. cot dot hot rot shot
4. feel heel meal seal zeal
5. chick lick pick sick tick
6. beat heat meet neat seat wheat
7. bed dead head led said wed

Unit 5

Listening Exercise 1

Modern life is full of hassles, demands, frustrations, and deadlines. For many people, stress is so commonplace that it has become a way of life.

Stress is the body's way of protecting you. When working properly, it helps you stay focused, energetic, and alert. In emergencies, stress can even save your life.

Stress also helps you rise to meet challenges. Stress is what keeps you on your toes during a presentation at work, sharpens your concentration when you're attempting the game-winning free throw, and drives you to study for an exam when you'd rather be watching TV. But beyond a certain point, stress stops being helpful and starts causing major damage to your health, your mood, your productivity, your relationships, and your life.

You may feel that the stress in your life is out of your control, but you can always control the way you respond to it. Managing stress is all about taking charge of your thoughts, your emotions, your schedule, your environment, and the way you deal with problems. Stress management involves changing the stressful situation when you can, changing your reaction when you can't, taking care of yourself, and finding the time for rest and relaxation.

To deal with stress effectively, you must learn to manage your relationships, your environment, your lifestyle, and your attitude.

To manage your attitude, you must

- avoid looking at people and things negatively
- control negative traits such as an inferiority complex, a lack of self esteem, perfectionism and apprehensiveness
- learn to view things that happen to you and in your society in a proper perspective
- prepare to modify your values as you learn from what you have read, observed and experienced

To manage your relationships, you must

- learn to be friendly and cooperative with people
- take delight in finding good things in other people rather than focusing on the bad
- learn to have assertive conversations with those who cause anxiety
- protect your personal freedom and space
- respect the views and rights of others
- share your worries with close ones
- participate in social service activities
- take the initiative in suggesting solutions to problems

To manage your environment, you must

- identify the things that cause you stress
- find ways to deal with them effectively
- surround yourself with things that relax you and fill you with positive thoughts
- find a time and place each day where you can have complete privacy

To manage your lifestyle, you must

- change your lifestyle by removing the causes of stress
- do physical exercises daily
- not depend on your peers to set standards for you
- get sufficient rest
- have enough time to pursue your hobbies
- learn to slow down by setting reasonable goals
- maintain a good diet
- practise relaxation
- take short breaks during your work

I hope what I have shared with you now will help you to manage stress effectively. Thank you, and good luck!

Listening Exercise 2

Teacher: Hello, Harish. You look tense today; what's the matter?

Harish: I need to give a presentation today and I'm very worried about it.

Teacher: Oh, I see. What's the venue, and when are you giving your presentation?

Harish: It's in the department's seminar hall at 3 p.m.

Teacher: How are you going to make your presentation?

Harish: I'm planning to make a PowerPoint presentation. I hope there won't be a power failure at that time.

Teacher: You should also be ready with your notes on some cue cards. And be prepared to use the whiteboard for your presentation.

Harish: Thank you for your advice. Can you please give me some more tips?

Teacher: Prepare the structure of your presentation carefully and logically. Think of the objectives of your presentation and the main points you want to make. Remember to rehearse your presentation to yourself at first and then in front of some classmates.

Harish: What can I do to overcome my stage fright?

Teacher: Channel your fear into energy. Appear confident and cheerful. Be energetic and enthusiastic. Use the right gesture at the right time. And you can be a little theatrical, but don't overdo it.

Harish: I'm also worried about my delivery of the presentation.

Teacher: Be natural without sounding conversational. Don't speak in a monotone; vary your speed and the pitch and tone of your voice. Do not speak too loudly or softly, but judge the acoustics of the room before you speak. Don't rush, but don't talk too slowly either. However, you can pause at key points for emphasis.

Harish: What about my language?

Teacher: Your language should be clear, concise, correct and courteous.

Harish: The thought of having to answer questions from the audience unnerves me.

Teacher: Stay cool and don't worry too much about it. Be sure to leave enough time for questions. Learn to handle negative questions. Be frank if you can't answer some questions. You can promise the person who asked you the question that you will get back to them after the presentation.

Harish: Another thought that gives me the jitters is how my presentation is going to be evaluated.

Teacher: Relax. We take into account things like the choice of topic, preparation, delivery, language, body language, time management, voice management, audience involvement and response to questions.

Harish: Thank you very much for all your suggestions.

Teacher: That's all right. Good luck for your presentation.

Listening Exercise 3

Listen to these words and repeat after the speaker.

1. a**lert**
2. be**come**
3. **cha**llenge
4. **da**mage
5. de**ligh**t
6. de**mand**
7. ener**ge**tic
8. **fo**cus
9. **mo**dern
10. **mo**dify
11. par**ti**cipate
12. **pe**ople
13. pre**pare**
14. produc**ti**vity
15. **qua**lity
16. re**move**
17. res**po**nse
18. **ser**vice
19. **so**cial
20. **va**lue

Listening Exercise 4

Listen to these sentences and repeat after the speaker. Note the intonation and rhythm.

1. **Mo**dern life is **full** of de**mands**.
2. **Str**ess has be**come** a **way** of **li**fe.
3. **St**ress helps you **stay fo**cused, ener**ge**tic, and a**le**rt.
4. The **str**ess response **h**elps you **rise** to **meet chal**lenges.
5. **St**ress can **da**mage your produc**ti**vity and **qua**lity of **life**.
6. Be pre**pare**d to **mo**dify your **va**lues.
7. Take de**li**ght in **fi**nding **go**od things in **oth**er **peo**ple.
8. Par**ti**cipate in **so**cial **ser**vice ac**ti**vities.
9. **Cha**nge your lifestyle by re**mov**ing the **cau**ses of **str**ess.
10. You must **le**arn to **cel**ebrate your **li**fe.

Unit 6

Listening Exercise 1

Student: Could you please tell me what interpersonal communication is?

Teacher: Interpersonal communication refers to your ability to relate yourself to people around you verbally and nonverbally.

Student: What should I do to be effective in interpersonal communication?

Teacher: You must possess the ability to deal with different people in different situations. Your interpersonal effectiveness is determined by how successful you are in different situations with different people.

Student: Can you give me some tips on interpersonal communication?

Teacher: You must change your pace, pitch and tone depending upon the situation. And also learn to use the right expression depending on the relationship you share with the person you are talking to. It's also a good idea to understand that topics of discussion change depending on the setting and the mood of the people involved in a conversation.

Student: Can you tell me about the functions of interpersonal communication?

Teacher: You can engage in interpersonal communication to learn about others, to establish your identity, to express interpersonal needs, and to build relations.

Student: Can you explain these in greater detail?

Teacher: Well, you often engage in interpersonal communication to gain knowledge about the people around you, so that you can interact with them more effectively. It can also help to establish your identity in the society around you, and to express and receive interpersonal needs like greetings, wishes, requests, orders, permissions, and complaints. Finally, through interpersonal communication, you develop better relationships with people. You can make friends and establish relationships depending on how successful you are as a communicator.

Student: Could you tell me about some conversational techniques?

Teacher: Remember that in most conversations, it is important to exchange greetings and pleasantries, and to talk about topics like the weather and current events. Ask easy questions to get the conversation going smoothly. Get to know about the hobbies, interests and topics of choice of other people, and try to talk about them.

Student: Any tips on how to close conversations?

Teacher: Well, indicate verbally and nonverbally that conversation is coming to an end. But make sure that you don't close a conversation abruptly. Let the people you are talking to know how you've enjoyed talking with them, and say that you'd like to meet them again.

Student: Thanks for sharing your ideas on interpersonal communication.

Teacher: You're welcome. Good luck!

Listening Exercise 2

In this short presentation, I shall cover the key listening strategies you need to develop your interpersonal skills. Good listening skills are vital for effective communication. You cannot become a successful communicator unless you are a good listener. However, listening is usually taken for granted. Research has shown that people listen with only 25 per cent efficiency. You must understand that listening is not just hearing. You hear when you only make out what the speaker says, but real listening involves understanding and evaluating what you hear. Let me now talk to you about ten important strategies for effective listening:

1. Listen for main ideas. As you listen, decide which information is vital and which is unnecessary. Focus mainly on the significant details.
2. Stay attentive. Involve yourself fully. Don't let your mind wander or be distracted. Concentrate on the speaker's words and body language. Maintain an active body state. If you are alert, it will be easier to fight any distractions.
3. Be genuinely interested in the other person and the message. If you are bored with the person and the message, it will definitely show in your body language and your replies.
4. Observe nonverbal cues like smiles, gestures, eye contact, and posture to help you go beyond what people say to understand what they really mean.
5. Give feedback verbally and nonverbally. Maintain eye contact with the speaker. Now and then, nod to show that you understand. Smile, laugh, or be silent as the occasion requires.
6. Focus on content and delivery. Listen not only to the words but also to the tone of voice.
7. Ask questions that will help you get the right response. The questions should help you get as much detail as you can from the person about the message. This means asking intelligent and pertinent questions.
8. Listen carefully. Do not finish the speaker's sentences. Do not interrupt incessantly. Let the speaker finish before you begin to talk. Very importantly, don't just keep yourself busy thinking about what you want to say next. Pay attention!
9. Don't allow yourself to get too emotional. Be objective and open-minded. Be aware of biases and perceptions. Control your biases and validate your assumptions. If the other party uses emotion-laden words, comprehend the message rather than reacting automatically. This will help defuse a potentially volatile situation.
10. Learn to empathize. Feel empathy for the other party when you are listening. You will be able to better understand what the other person is saying if do.

I'd like all of you to follow these ten strategies of effective listening and become successful in your everyday interactions with people. This brings my presentation to a close. Thank you very much for your time.

Listening Exercise 3

Listen to these words and repeat after the speaker.

Vowel sounds

Symbol/Sound	Keyword
/ə /	about
/ɑ:/	ask
/ɪ/	it
/i:/	eat
/ʊ/	pull
/u:/	pool
/e/	pen
/æ/	pat
/ʌ/	cut
/ɜ:/	girl
/ɒ /	cot
/ɔ:/	caught
/eɪ/	say
/aɪ/	ice
/ɔɪ/	boy
/ɪə/	dear
/eə/	fair
/ʊə/	poor
/aʊ/	out
/əʊ/	go

Consonant sounds

Symbol/Sound	Keyword
/p/	pack
/b/	back
/t/	ten
/d/	den
/tʃ/	cheap
/dʒ/	jeep
/k/	kit
/g/	get
/f/	fan
/v/	van
/θ/	thin
/ð/	then
/m/	meet
/n/	neat
/ŋ/	bank
/h/	hat
/s/	seat
/z/	zoo
/ʃ/	ship
/ʒ/	pleasure
/r/	read
/l/	lead
/j/	yet
/w/	wet

Listening Exercise 4

You need to know about two kinds of sounds that affect -ed and -s/-es pronunciations.

1. The first kind are **voiceless sounds**, which are made by pushing air through your mouth. No sound comes from the throat.

   s - x - c - ch - sh - p - k - f - q - gh are examples of voiceless sounds.

2. The second kind or sounds are voiced sounds come from the throat, that is, the voice vibrates in the neck.

   d - b - r - l - m - n - v are examples of voiced sounds.

Listen to these words that end with -ed and -s/-es and note the pronunciation:

booked	bagged	batted
books	bags	buses

-ed is pronounced as /t/ after all voiceless sounds except /t/.

clapped	/klæpt/
missed	/mɪst/
crushed	/krʌʃt/
reached	/ri:tʃt/

-ed is pronounced as /d/ after all voiced sounds except /d/.

dragged	/drægd/
fried	/fraɪd/
cleaned	/kli:nd/
summed	/sʌmd/
cured	/kjuəd/
loved	/lʌvd/
curbed	/kɜ:bd/

-ed is pronounced as /id/ after /t/ and /d/.

painted	/peɪntɪd/
wanted	/wɔ:ntɪd
sounded	/saʊndɪd/
grounded	/graʊndɪd/

Listen to these words that end with -s and -es and note the pronunciation:

-s is pronounced as /s/ after all voiceless sounds except /s/, /ʃ/ and /tʃ/

caps	/kæps/
writes	/raɪts/
laughs	/lɑ:fs/
picks	/pɪks/
hits	/hɪts/
pats	/pæts/

-s is pronounced as /z/ after all voiced sounds except /z/, /ʒ/ and /dʒ/

rags	/rægz/
toys	/tɔɪz/
friends	/frendz/
ends	/endz/
dreams	/dri:mz/
legs	/legz/
cleans	/kli:nz/
fans	/fænz/

-es is pronounced as /ɪz/ after /s/, /ʃ/, /tʃ/, /z/, /ʒ/ and / dʒ/

places	/pleɪsɪz/
crushes	/krʌʃɪ z/
searches	/sɜ:tʃɪz/

Listening Exercise 5

Listen to these words and note the -ed pronunciations.

1. Vandana visit**ed** many places.
2. She work**ed** in a reput**ed** organization.
3. They've demolish**ed** many buildings.
4. They clean**ed** some lakes and rivers.
5. We watch**ed** many movies.

Unit 7

Listening Exercise 1

Student: I need some help, ma'am. Could you please tell me what time management is.

Teacher: Well, simply put, time management means making the best use of the time that's available to you.

Student: Why is time management important?

Teacher: Time management can help you to achieve personal and professional success. You can complete your tasks in time and learn to enjoy your life to the most by managing your time effectively.

Student: Could I know how to manage my time effectively?

Teacher: To manage your time effectively, you need to focus on being productive, not just busy. The secret to making the best use of the time is to concentrate on the things that matter the most and be as result-oriented as you can.

Student: What are the methods or principles that I should follow?

Teacher: There are many methods and principles. For now, I'll talk about the Pareto principle and the P-O-S-E-C POSEC method.

Student: What are they?

Teacher: The Pareto principle, or the 80:20 rule, states that that for many events, roughly 80 per cent of the effects come from 20 per cent of the causes. In other words, typically 80 per cent of unfocused effort generates only 20 per cent of results. The remaining 80 per cent of results are achieved with only 20 per cent of the effort. When applied to time management and your daily to-do list, it means that 80 per cent of your measurable results and progress will come from just 20 per cent of the items on your daily to-do list.

Student: Does this mean that of the things I do during my day, only 20 per cent really matter?

Teacher: Exactly. Identify and focus on the 20 per cent that produces 80 per cent of your results. If something in the schedule has to slip, if something isn't going to get done, make sure it's not part of that 20 per cent.

Student: So, I shouldn't just be working hard throughout the day but instead focus on doing the right things.

Teacher: Yes, you should concentrate most of your time and energy on the high pay-off tasks.

Student: What is the POSEC method?

Teacher: P-O-S-E-C POSEC stands for P- Prioritize by O- Organizing, S- Streamlining, E- Economizing and C- Contributing. Prioritize your time and define your life by goals. Organize things you have to accomplish regularly. Streamline your work and other chores so that you can move quickly and effectively. Economize, or spend less time, on things that you should do or may even like to do, but that aren't very urgent. Contribute by paying attention to the few remaining things that make a difference, like fulfilling your social obligations.

Student: What does all this mean?

Teacher: It means that by attending to one's personal responsibilities first, an individual is better positioned to shoulder collective responsibilities.

Student: Thank you for sharing your valuable knowledge on time management.

Teacher: I hope you'll use this knowledge to make the best use of your time and accomplish your tasks in an effective manner.

Listening Exercise 2

Hello. In this short presentation, I shall focus on some aspects related to managing your time. These include understanding the value of time, understanding how you lose your time and learning to optimize your time.

Let me talk to you about the value of time. You'll be more conscious about managing your time once you realize how important time is. Time is the most valuable resource available to all of you. However, most of you take it for granted and are not aware how it can be used to achieve success.

You all know the famous proverb "Time and tide wait for none". This means that you should act without delay. Ask yourself if you postpone things unnecessarily.

Making the best use of time involves understanding how you waste your time or what your 'time robbers' are. Some of the time robbers for many people include:

- Lack of clear planning
- Not prioritizing tasks
- Not taking the right decisions
- Procrastinating
- Chatting and gossiping for too long
- Watching too much TV

Ask yourselves what your time robbers are. Once you are ready with your own list of time robbers, you must make conscious effort to reduce or overcome them.

I'd now like to focus on helping you to optimize your time. To optimize your time, you should

- have clear written goals
- use to-do lists
- prioritize things
- use diaries, planners, track sheets, or digital pocket organizers
- make the right decisions at the right time
- review your actions periodically
- work smarter, not harder

In conclusion, I'd like to say that you have enough time to rest, to get things done, and to know how you've done them. You can be more productive and more relaxed using the points I've just presented. This brings my presentation to a close. Thank you very much for your time and cooperation.

Listening Exercise 3

Listen to the full forms of these words and their contracted forms and repeat after the speaker.

I am	I'm
I have	I've
I will	I'll
I would/I had	I'd
it is/it has	it's
it will	it'll
it would/it had	it'd
he is/he has	he's
he will	he'll
he would/he had	he'd
she is/she has	she's
she will	she'll
she would/she had	she'd
they are	they're
they have	they've
they will	they'll
they would/they had	they'd
we are	we're
we have	we've
we would/we had	we'd
you are	you're
you have	you've
you will	you'll
you would/you had	you'd
are not	aren't

cannot	can't
could not	couldn't
dare not	daren't
did not	didn't
do not	don't
does not	doesn't
had not	hadn't
has not	hasn't
have not	haven't
is not	isn't
must not	mustn't
need not	needn't
ought not	oughtn't
shall not	shan't
should not	shouldn't
was not	wasn't
will not	won't
would not	wouldn't

Listening Exercise 4

Listen to these sentences and repeat after the speaker. Note how certain words are contracted in pronunciation.

1. **I'd** like to work in a focused and effective way to accomplish my high-pay-off tasks.
2. Dinesh **doesn't** fritter his time away on conflicting priorities.
3. **She's** worked on strategically important tasks.
4. **We've** leant techniques to minimize the interruptions.
5. **He'd** rewarded himself for completing high-priority tasks in time.
6. **They've** devised ways to beat procrastination.
7. **He's** good at scheduling his time effectively.
8. I **don't** normally over-commit to others.
9. **I've** realized that careless decisions could kill time.